Signed with an X

Based on a true story

J.A. KAHN

PAGE PUBLISHING, INC.
Conneaut Lake, PA

First originally published by Page Publishing 2021

ISBN 978-1-6624-3393-1 (pbk)
ISBN 978-1-6624-3394-8 (digital)

Printed in the United States of America

ACKNOWLEDGMENTS

THANK YOU, BRAUM Katz, my awesome grandson, for keeping me on track. Your eternal patience, love, technical expertise, and most especially your ongoing assurances of "I have your back, Grandma!"

My gratitude to Lynn Spain for editing and keeping me focused.

To Professor Gordy Beaver, who asked me about my background and when I emailed this unfinished saga to him, his interest was profound.

To Angie Silver, for her memory of our shared times.

To Alice Greenspan, Pam Mayer, Sue Greenberg, Naomi Friedman, Rich Bergman and Ernestine Martinez for their guidance and encouragement. And thanks to Al Klomparens for help with the final edits.

INTRODUCTION

My Father Remembered

WE OPENED HIS desk drawer when my father died. There was a letter written on behalf of the Israeli government signed by Brigadier-General Ezer Weizman thanking Daddy for arranging for guns bought in Czechoslovakia to be sent to Israel.

We also found my father's birth certificate. Upon entering England, my grandfather had signed it with an *X*. Evidently, he could not read or write English. Fifty years later, I realized customs had replaced his actual birth name, Josekovitch, with Lakin. Thus, my father was named Joseph Lakin.

RE: VE and VJ days

VE Day (Victory in Europe Day) was May 8, 1945, in the Allied countries. VJ Day was August 15, 1945, but September 2, 1945, the day the Japanese signed for unconditional surrender is also known as VJ Day (Victory over Japan Day).

I remember the night the lights were turned on at Piccadilly Circus. We stood around holding hands and singing "Should Old Acquaintance Be Forgot" with tears in our eyes as we felt the love of total strangers standing next to us.

For information on precisely when these were announced to the English public, I would suggest looking in the *Times* newspaper around those dates. (My guess, however, is that the initial announcement would have been by radio.)

CHAPTER 1

Dinner with Daddy, 1948

A KIPPER LAYS on a plate awaiting my father. It is burnt just enough to cause the crispy skeletal system to peel away from the flesh. Beside the kipper is a braised tomato and a slice of buttered bread. This is my father's evening meal. I love kippers. There is one for me too. I am eleven years old.

When we are seated, Ilsa, the housekeeper, brings in the silver tea service. Ilsa is a German refugee. She is tall and stately and perfectly costumed in her white ruffled apron over the black uniform, the perfect match for the Queen Ann tea service. A pot of tea, a pot of hot water, a small pitcher of milk, a dish of white sugar cubes, and a strainer on the side. My father pours the milk into the cup, strains the tea while almost filling the cup, topping it off with hot water. He then fills the cup with sugar cubes until one is visible above the tea line. A combination of Russian and English sweet-tooth habits will shorten his life.

We are comfortably seated in our red leather high-back chairs. Their carved light wood frames add a sturdy support for our nightly visit to the terrors that remain a mystery.

My parents are divorced. My father now sits with me long hours into the night talking about Jewish history and WWII. He describes the foreboding pictures he had seen in the *Daily Express* as Germany prepared for invasion. I can still hear the fear in his voice as he says,

"There had never been anything like it, you could see soldiers coming like great waves. Soldiers and more soldiers, covering the ground as far as the eye could see, evil-looking armored tanks with squared-off impenetrable moving robotic guns. Everyone knew that England had nothing like it and wasn't even making any attempt to defend herself."

My eyes wander around his flat. I stare at the colored glass monkeys on the mantel, "Hear no evil, speak no evil, see no evil," each monkey dressed in formal attire of darkly stained glass. The war talk is entrenched in my being. My father describes how he would listen to the static-filled nightly radio reports, fine-tuning the knobs in search of news.

"We heard rumors of Jewish death camps and we knew how vulnerable the Jewish community would be, should England fall to the Germans," he recalls.

My peace-loving daddy joined the Irgun, the Jewish underground movement. The idea was to keep an eye on anti-Semitism in England. He walked a fine line between his country and his heritage. He was first-generation English. After he died, I found his birth certificate. His parents were from Kiev. They had escaped the pogroms in Russia. Neither one could read or write English. I never met my grandfather; he died before I was born, but my grandmother spoke fluent English with a Slavic accent. I was shocked to see my father's birth certificate signed with an *X*.

Every Friday, being Shabbat, at the family gathering at my grandma's house, someone would fumble with the radio trying to pick up news of the British rule in Palestine. They would gasp as one as they listened to reports of the English troops brutalizing Jews attempting to immigrate to Palestine.

Stories of a future state for the Jews were my bedtime stories. At an early age, I knew that Hitler hated me especially. No matter how good I was, or how pretty, he still hated me. Because I was Jewish. I remember thinking, *If Hitler knew me, I was sure he wouldn't hate me. Why won't he just meet me and then decide?*

When I questioned my father about the Holocaust, he always assured me that "the world will remember." After this, Jews would have a place where they would be safe. Then he taught me about Chaim Weizmann, who, by finding a way to mass-produce acetone, had helped England develop gunpowder for the war effort. In return for that gift, during WWI, England would turn Palestine over to the Jews.

So, between Moses and the parting of the Dead Sea, Judas Maccabeus and the rebuilding of the Temple, I could add Chaim Wiezmann to winning back our homeland. But still, my childhood was plagued with dreams of murderous men hating me, chasing me, from room to room.

CHAPTER 2

Mum's Story, in Her Own Words

IN 1940, WE were on holiday at Sandbanks on the coast of England. I had an argument with the nanny. I told her to leave. She didn't. Then your father phoned. "Don't come home," he said. "I've rented another place. The people want to rent it out if there is a war. They want it for themselves if there isn't."

I wrote to my mother (my grandma) and invited her to come to stay. She was so thrilled that I wanted to get her out of London that she read my letter to her niece, Netta.

Netta's husband had been called up on the first day of the war, so Netta appeared at Sandbanks, uninvited, with her tiny infant. After a few days, when your father had come down for a weekend visit, he wasn't exactly thrilled with the living space. He went out and managed to find a room for Netta. She could sleep there but continue to eat with us. Our maid, a German refugee, a cultured lady who had fled Germany, was sleeping on the sofa in the dining room. Even though Netta ate all her meals with us, and Joe (my father) was paying for her room, that wasn't good enough!

(This is how my mother dealt with the potential German invasion of England. It is mostly in her own words. She was in her eighties when I began to write.)

It was 1940 when we heard the guns. We were away when Chamberlain, the prime minister, waved that sheet of paper in the air while declaring, "Peace in our time." We had gone away because we thought there was going to be a war. We sold the house at Talbot Crescent; it had such a lovely rose garden. You were born in that house. We had left London again and were on holiday in Worthing with the Bernards (my father's business partner's wife and their two children].

Worthing is on the coast of England, and the house we were renting was very close to the water. They were shelling across the Channel in France, but when I said "I can hear guns," Dora Bernard said, "No, that's not gunfire, that's the wind."

I said, "That is guns, I know a gun when I hear it." We read about it in the paper the next day. We went back to the house, and I think we went back to London to pack before we left for Cullompton, Devon, with Aylsa. (That was Aylsa Cohen, my mother's best friend and her daughters, Angela [Angie] and Jaquelin [Jackie].)

It was the middle of the summer. The coast guards were shooting planes down in Hyde Park. They were bombing all over the place; nowhere was safe when we left. We'd hear the planes at night. They'd come in from Germany flying over to bomb the Bristol Channel.

Every night, I had the same dream. There were Nazis at my door coming to arrest me. When Churchill gave his famous speech, "We'll fight them in the trenches," you were pushing your toy pram, and I was listening to the radio. I remember I was standing up, and I was crying as I listened. I was so impressed with his speech. We were going to fight on and on. We certainly were not winning at the time. We would fight to the last man as it was. I didn't know we would be leaving England then. It was after that, that I got the call.

We were with the nanny when your father phoned. He said, "We've got a chance for you to go to America."

I told him, "I don't want to go to America."

He had made up his mind. "I want you to go. I've already spoken to Nat (Cohen). We want you and Aylsa (Cohen, Mum's close friend) to go with the children." So I went back to London. We were staying at the Mount Royal Hotel near Piccadilly Circus. We girls had lunch with our two mothers at John Lewis's Restaurant. Both our mothers agreed that they didn't want us to go, but we should in order to protect the children, as we would be safe in America.

(I asked Mum, "What about the journey?") Everybody knew that the water was dangerous, but it was the only way. Women and children were not being transported by plane at that time.

We had heard about Jewish concentration camps in Germany. We knew what was going on over there. I would wake up terrified night after night after my dream, and I think, now that I look back, that made it easier to leave England. Joe (my father) explained to me that if Hitler invaded England, maybe alone he could get away, but with the three of us, chances were that we couldn't get away.

We had a lot of discussions when we returned from Devon. We were told we had to get visas and sign for them.

We were booked on the Duchess of Atholl. It was part of the Canadian Pacific Line and had been put to war work. All the people who were leaving England had had to get a visa, the American embassy was too small to accommodate all the people, so they were using the ballroom of the Grosvenor House Hotel. It was the largest ballroom in England. We were lucky; we had connections. Nat knew someone in the film business, so we did not have to sleep in the corridors to wait in line. It had been prearranged by Joe Kennedy's son, the one who was in the film business. Nat had also arranged for Sam Goldwyn to send a sponsor letter. (Nat Cohen, or Uncle Nat, as I knew him, was well-known as a British movie producer.)

Uncle Nat with Prince Philip at a Variety Club celebration

CHAPTER 3

Crossing the Atlantic 1940

WE LEFT FOR America right after the Battle of Britain. Our journey started in July. We bought all new clothes; our husbands had told us to go out and buy anything we wanted. Of course, when you have that kind of an invitation, you really don't know what you want. Sylvia (Mum's friend) came with me to shop, and we were in Gallery Lafayette in Regent Street, and my handbag disappeared. It had a pendant crystal watch and all the family pictures that I had wanted to take with me. I went to the police station, and I was told, "We have hundreds of reports of these every day, but thank you for letting us know."

The day we were to leave England, we all took the train from London to Liverpool together—the Cohen family, Aylsa and Nat, with their two daughters, Jackie, age seven, Angie, age four, and you, age two, your father, and me. The Duchess of Atholl left from Liverpool. As we got off the train to get on the ship, there was an air-raid warning; the sirens went off. As soon as the all-clear sounded, we were hurriedly herded on to the waiting ship with no time for a real goodbye.

As we reached the deck, I could see your father anxiously pointing to your furry toy lion. It had a loose eye and a hairy long black mane. It was both a toy and a pajama case, with a zipper running down the lion's back. Your father was frantically pointing to it and mouthing that you had left it. Actually, it was more important than it looked because it looked like, and was, a cuddly toy. It was also my emergency bank for this journey. It housed my diamond bracelet which was our insurance in case we ran short of money. Joe was able to persuade an attendant to take the lion on board and give it to me for "his little girl."

The ship immediately began to pull away from the dock. We only had time to wave and mouth our goodbyes. We stared after them, wondering what was ahead for each of us. If we would see our parents again. I wondered about my sister, Bea, and Joe (my father). What would become of us? We watched them for as long as we could, then we went to settle into the cabins. Our cabin had three bunks— one above the other, and one underneath the window which is where Nat's partner, Jerry Rafer's sister, slept. So many young Jewish men were killed during the war. Sylvia had two brothers who were in the air force and were shot down. One was shot as he was parachuting from the plane. Both were killed. I remember what naughty little boys they were!

Sol Yager had a plane, and he flew out and signaled us goodbye because Etty Yager (his wife) and their son were with us on the ship.

It took the ship a week to reach Montreal. We had been told we would have an escort for protection for the journey. A plane did fly along with us the first day, but only for that day. The next day, it peeled away to return to England and we were on our own. Everybody knew we had no escort and no guns; we were all worried and nervous. Once we settled down, it wasn't quite what we expected. All the time, you could hear children crying. It never stopped. We had been told it was a big ship and children needed to know their full names. One day, a nice man said to you, "Hello, my little ray of sunshine."

You answered, "I'm not your little ray of sunshine, I'm Janice Andrea Lakin." So much for teaching you your whole name! The boat was full of young children except for a few people traveling over to America on business. The sky was reserved for warfare at that time, so everyone else traveled by ship.

Once on board, you didn't eat anything, just tasted the food.

Mum in her beaver coat

The Cohen kids ate everything in sight. We were too scared to even think about being scared. It was much more scary on the ship than staying home in London.

I had bought a beaver coat during our shopping spree, and when we got to America, a lot of moths flew out of the trunk but I couldn't see where they had eaten anything so I wasn't worried. We knew that in America, the winters were severe and the summers were hotter than England.

Aylsa and Elsie, known as the two Elsies

After we unpacked, we went to the dining area to select a table where we would eat our meals.

We had our own three little girls and another young girl who was the younger sister of Nat's partner. We were to deliver her to a family in Montreal. We brought her back to England with us when we returned. By then, Nat's partner, who was on leave, had been killed when the Germans bombed the Café de Paris. Everybody thought the Café de Paris was safe because it was underground, but there was no building above it to protect it. It was full of our friends. I wish I could remember their names. (The Cafe de Paris was later rebuilt, but the night it was bombed was mentioned throughout my childhood. My dad took me there to see Shirley Bassy, who later would receive the award for Best British Female Solo Artist. I was eighteen.

It was a bittersweet evening, as my father recalled the bombing that night, too.)

We all knew that most of the ships that left England had had escorts.

After we pulled out of port, it was tense the whole time. We were always on alert to put on our life jackets, but we would have been an easy target because we were just a big ship crossing the Atlantic alone. (The Duchess of Atholl was 20,119 tons, 581 feet long by 75 feet wide at waterline. Driven by steam turbines, she had two masts and two funnels and carried 580 cabin-class passengers, 480 tourist class, and 510 in third class. She was launched on July 13, 1928, and her maiden voyage was from Liverpool to Quebec and Montreal. She was torpedoed and sunk in the South Atlantic on a voyage from the Near East to England on October 10, 1942.) I began to have terrible stomach pain, so Aylsa insisted I see the ship's doctor. He said it was my appendix. He put me in the ship's hospital, which was a room with only a couple of beds.

I spent the night there. Aylsa looked after you and put you to bed. And the next day, they were going to operate. Well, the ship was hooting and honking a peculiar noise. All of a sudden, it stopped. It just stopped moving. I thought, *This is it. They're coming in with the knife to operate on me.* Then the doctor came in and said, "Don't worry, we've stopped because we've sighted an iceberg."

I was left lying there waiting for surgery for another few hours. When the doctor came back in, he said, "If you can possibly get up, get up because we're nearly there, and I have had to put two children in sanatorium because they have the measles, and, if you're in the same room with them I will have to put you in quarantine and you, and the children, will have to stay on board after everybody else has departed."

So I said, "I think I can get up now." So I got up. I believe it was another day before we reached Montreal. The pain came back once after we got home to London and one more time after that. I expect it was just nerves.

We had been out at sea quite a while. We were closer to Canada than England. The ship stopped, and they made some excuse. They had let off a depth charge. Afterward, I noticed there was debris float-ing on the water. I could see bits of wood and bits of steel that looked like machinery. They did not tell us anything; it was never men-tioned. After all, it was a British ship.

CHAPTER 4

Safe but Where's Harry?

WHEN WE ARRIVED in Montreal, it was about five in the morning. We were told that Sam Beckman (my father's close friend) was waiting for us, but they couldn't let him come aboard because of the war. I had been holding you for some time, you were heavy because I was also holding another bag and papers for traveling, and you were squirming while they made sure we weren't spies. They let a few spies off that ship, mind you. We spent that day at the Beckman's. We discussed what to do next. We decided to go directly to New York. Sam took an earlier train because he couldn't get a seat on our train. He was there to meet us when we got to New York. He suggested, since we didn't know where we were going to stay, that we stay at his hotel. You started screaming, "I want to go on the beach." You had been on a ship and a train, and the only time you'd ever been on a train before was to go to the beach. After we unpacked, we took you all out to keep you quiet.

We did stay at Sam's hotel, Park Central, and then I had to start to search for Harry Massey. Harry had money for me. I began by phoning one or two English people that we knew to see if they knew where he was living. They suggested that we try Essex House, and he was there, and he was amazed that I found him. I don't think he lived there. I think he was just with somebody. I said, "I know that some money has been transferred to you."

He said, "That's true, but that money is not for you, that's for Joe."

And I said, "Don't be ridiculous, you know very well it's for me and the baby. Why do you think he sent it here? Joe can't stand the baby to go without anything. If he thought his daughter would have to go without a bar of chocolate, he wouldn't have sent us here."

He said, "You'd better come and see me." So I took Sam Beckman with me, and he said to Harry, "You know that money is for Elsie and the baby." He gave me a $100.

Harry then said, "If Joe came here, I'd be a gentleman."

Sam said, "That remains to be discussed."

Joe had given a relative of Harry's who lived in England about £5000. Harry was already in America and £5000 pounds was more like £25,000 ($50,000) in today's money.

It was illegal to take money out of England, and so paying in pounds and receiving in dollars enabled us to survive in America. I don't think Harry paid Joe back that money for many, many years. In the end, Joe said he forgave Harry because he taught him everything he knew in business. (Daddy had worked for [Harry] Ornstein and Massoff before he opened his own business, which he opened the day he turned twenty-one because before that, the bank would not accept his signature.) Aylsa had got some money, and before we left England, our two husbands had made an agreement that we girls should share everything, I don't think we put it in a bank; we kept it all in cash, all together, so that whoever got money, it just went into the kitty. The next week, somebody phoned me—a friend of Joe's. He took me to the opera. He took me to a birthday dinner for the chairman of the Chase Bank; it was at the Pierre Hotel. I got all dressed up. I wore a long black crepe dress, with an emerald green bolero with a border of colorful flowers that was printed on the dress, and I perspired so much that I ruined the dress, and it turned out that I had pleurisy.

I had to stay in bed for several days. I don't think we had met Sidney Steckel yet, so he wasn't our doctor. Sidney never charged us when he came because he felt it was his contribution to the war effort. Any rate, the opera, *Lucia di Lammermoor*, was a French interpretation of a story that took place in Scotland, very unusual, and it was at the old opera house in New York. Monday night was the chic night to go. I thought we were going to the plaza afterward, but in the middle of the opera, they brought a horse on the stage, and I gasped and sneezed, and they had to take me home. Aylsa was home playing bridge with a man. I can't remember his name, but he invited me to go to Aldrich's. He was the chairman of the bank the Rothschilds own. He didn't give me money that night, but he did give me money on several occasions whenever the deal was made through London. I did get that money. The next time he invited me out, it was for dinner at the Pierre Hotel for Rockefeller's cousin who was having his seventieth birthday and was head of the Chase Bank. The next day, to my surprise, I received flowers from a couple of the people who had been there, just sent to make us feel welcome.

Aylsa and I decided that we needed some time together without the children, and that it would be a good thing if we could find someone who could walk them to the park. We found Iris. Her parents were French, but she was American.

We found a residential hotel on West Seventy-Second street, and we got an apartment on a high floor, and when we found out that it was cheaper to be on a lower floor, we moved. But we hadn't reckoned on the electric bill being so much higher on a lower floor. It was much darker in the apartment, and so we had to keep the lights on all day. Then we all moved to an apartment on Eighty-Sixth Street.

Once, I was wheeling you along when you first came to America, you became very excited and said, "Look, Mummy, there's a blue man." It was the first time you had seen a Black man.

You had a habit of making scenes when there were plenty of people around. Sidney Steckel wanted you to see a friend of his who was a psychiatrist. We took you to his friend's home because he didn't want you to know that he was a psychiatrist. He gave you all sorts of tests and then he said the shock of finding yourself suddenly with two older children caused you to be too competitive because those kids knew how to schmooze to everybody. Angie would open those big blue eyes and cry when somebody was leaving, but what they didn't realize was that she did it to everybody. So everybody made a big fuss of Angie and ignored you. I think that hurt me more than it hurt you, I don't think you gave a damn.

CHAPTER 5

The How-tos of $$$$

WHEN WE FIRST got to the hotel, maybe a week after we arrived in America, there was a phone call from a man from customs. He said he would come to see me; supposedly since I had a young child, he wouldn't put me to the trouble of going there. It was something about a baby carriage that I had with me. He didn't give me a real reason for coming, and we had already been through customs three times: once to get on the boat in Liverpool, then again to get off the boat in Montreal, then to get off the train in New York. I became nervous, so I phoned Sam Beckman, who was still in New York. I asked him what to do. Sam said, "Don't worry about it, he may just think he's being nice. Just make sure you're not in the room alone with him." It turned out that he was a perfectly nice man who really was concerned that the pram had not been damaged by rough handling on the train.

I was feeling so guilty about the jewelry, and most of those customs people were really hard on us coming in. When I had you in my arms, they went through every little piece of paper, even my address book, and anything they could find of personal interest. They had been quite indifferent to the crying babies. In Liverpool, when we left, they were the worst of all. All the people who were leaving were leaving with babies, and they treated us as though we were spies. The British government had encouraged anyone who could go to

24

America to go. There were people who lived in the country who took people in, just to get them out of London. Some of them were treated very well and remain friends to this day, and others had a very different story.

You see, we all thought it was very possible that the Germans would occupy England, and there was a chance for a single male to escape, but a man with a wife and family would have a much harder time of it.

Sam Beckman was the only person you would go to and who could quiet you down. After Uncle Sid (Mum's mum, Grandma Gilbert's sister Annie's husband) arrived, he was staying at the hotel on Forty-Second Street. He phoned me and said he'd like to see me. Sam Beckman said he'd like to meet him. It was good for Sam's business, as he sold fabric, and Sid was a very successful coat manufacturer. Sid was in America on business. This was smiled upon by the government because export was good for the economy. I got Sam and Sid together with the idea that Sid could influence Harry Massey to honor his agreement, since both men were in the coat business. I just thought maybe Sid could get through to Harry. Sid's response was, "I don't understand those kinds of arrangements at all." Of course he did because his own daughter, Zelda (Mum's cousin), had recently arrived in New York with her young daughter, and "those kind of arrangements" were the only way you could survive without earning a living. He refused to help. In order to avoid hard feelings, Uncle Sid invited me to go to a ball at the Waldorf Astoria. I gave him our address but, unfortunately, we lived on West Sixty-Fourth Street, and he went to East Sixty-Fourth Street which is where Mrs. Roosevelt had a house. It was at her house that Sid found himself. He eventually found our apartment, and we went to the ball. He introduced me as his niece, and I knew nobody believed him as I think his reputation as a ladies' man had preceded him across the ocean. For some reason, he took me instead of his girlfriend that night.

We lived in a state of concern about the people we had left behind.

At one time, they bombed a town where Aylsa's brother was living. We had devised a code to communicate about money. We would send a telegram using a family member name according to the number in the alphabet. It went like this: "Auntie Edna is much better" meant we could expect a, b, c, d, e…$500 soon. We would telegram back, "So happy to hear Auntie Edna is better." That meant the money had been delivered.

One day, a rabbi came to the door and said he wanted to see me. I was in bed. I had the flu. Aylsa said, "You can't see her, she's in bed."

He said, "I don't care, I have to see her." So I crawled out of bed. I could barely speak. He gave me about $1000. That's one thing I must say; your father found a way whenever he could. The deal was it had to be cash. I have no idea how it turned into dollars. None of us knew. None of us wanted to know, either. We were people who never wanted to be dishonest. Some people just promised to pay and did, in fact, pay after the war. There were some very wealthy Americans who did bring English families over and I think that was why many people returned to England during the war; they felt they were imposing after America entered.

CHAPTER 6

Missing Papers

WE MOVED INTO the Franconia; that was the name of the residential hotel. I don't think it had a restaurant, but they cleaned the rooms and changed the sheets. After that, we decided we had better go to something more practical. Dick Michaels lived in the same hotel. He became my friend, Sylvia's boyfriend many years later. He was in the movie business, and he used to babysit. He'd just sit and read his book at our place. In those days, you didn't think about the terrible things that could happen to children; it just didn't happen. I remember the first job I ever had. The man was touching me all the time. I only stayed there a week; I couldn't stand it.

We moved out of the Franconia to Sixty-Fourth Street. Anyway, the reason we moved was because we could get a very short lease there, and in the summer, we took a bungalow at Long Beach in Long Island. The Austins—they owned a men's store of that name in New York and London—had a bungalow there, and Mick Hyams (a movie associate of Uncle Nat) came to stay with them. By then, we knew several English people, so it seemed very convenient for our friends to come out for the day. Since these friends often brought their friends, we always had a full house. Aylsa did the cooking, and I tidied up the place, until one day when I was setting the table, I heard one of them say, "Who is she?" So I put my foot down after that and told Aylsa we weren't going to serve people we didn't know.

I brought you into town because you were having ear aches and they said you needed your tonsils out. So I went to a tonsil specialist, and I arranged that we would stay overnight at Sally's—I can't remember her name, but her husband was the first coat manufacturer to go "public" (that is, put his business in the stock market), but that was after the war. Mick Hyams had relatives in America, and he invited us to visit his cousins. They had farm eggs there; they sold them. I suggested that I could help them to distribute them. It never occurred to me to make a profit on it. I just sold them for what they asked and gave them all the money. Then someone said, "Imagine, now she's down to selling eggs." That was it, they could eat stale eggs if they wanted. I stopped. I just didn't have anything else to do.

One minute, it looked as though the war would end, the next minute it was on again. We realized that we had to decide what to do. We could go into business. We agreed about what the business would be; I would make hats and Aylsa would sell them. We could have rented a little place on Madison Avenue. We said, "If we can't get on a ship this summer, that's what we will do."

Fundraising for Bundles for Britain with
Ethel Merman in Central Park, NYC

The way to get home was on a Portuguese ship. There were a lot of women with children who decided to return home at this time.

America was at war. You came and told us that Sunday afternoon. You said, "Pull the blinds down, the Japanese are coming." You had heard about Pearl Harbor. One of our friends, a woman, decided we should all go to Pinehurst in North Carolina together, as it would be safer than staying in New York which was such an obvious target for bombs. Several of us decided we might just as well be in England where we belong.

Aylsa and I went to the tax office near Grand Central Station somewhere. We both had been given these pieces of paper that were exit permits. I had suggested to Aylsa that we put both papers together in her case because it had a lock on it. Very stupid of me. (Why that sounds sensible to me.) Anybody could take the whole thing out. Anyway, when Aylsa opened it to get the papers out because we were packing to leave, mine wasn't there. (What do you think happened to it?) I've wondered all these years.

I was advised to take you with me to see the exit people. I did take you. I said to them, "I can't find it. I can't find it anywhere. I'm desperate. I've already got the booking on the Serpa Pinto." I don't think anyone had brought a person of your age with them before, because they went out and brought ice cream and lollipops for you and made such a fuss of you. And they gave me a new exit permit.

CHAPTER 7

Aboard the Serpa Pinto 1943

WE SAILED FROM Philadelphia. We then had a lovely house-keeper. Her son was a musician in a band. She did this because she wanted to be with people, hated to be alone. She came with us to Philadelphia. She cried because we were leaving. She already had another job. When we got to Philadelphia, there were a whole lot of things that looked like snakes in the water. They were submarines. They were parked in the dock. It was a beautiful day that day, the end of August. It took us a week coming over from England, so we thought it would probably be about that going home, but we were in the water for two weeks.

When we got on board, the first thing we saw was an oversized Portuguese flag. It was painted on a huge wall made of wooden slats, and it had great big lights focused on it. That was to let everyone know they were Portuguese, and they were a neutral country. We couldn't go back on an English ship then.

(The Serpa Pinto was owned by Compahia colonial De Navgacao. It was built in 1915 in Ireland and was 8,267 tons, 450 feet long and 57 feet wide, with twin propellers, quadruple expansion engines, two masts, one funnel. It was capable of doing 14 knots, and its route was from Lisbon to Santos. It was scrapped in 1955.)

The food was quite good if you felt like eating, which the Cohen kids did and, of course, you didn't. Everybody got seasick at some time. There was a fierce storm at sea. They didn't warn us. We had had boat drills before, but they didn't suggest using the boats.

They had put up ropes everywhere as the storm approached, and they took all the smaller children into a lounge area that was sheltered by other areas of the ship, and they told us to give the children a toy or a book to read. They told the kids to lie down on the floor and play with their dolls or read their books. The adults, well, we just sat where we could. You couldn't walk without holding on to a rope. Aylsa didn't feel good. I felt okay, remarkably, if a trifle nervous. Actually, I was frightened out of my life.

The Cohen girls were hungry, so they went downstairs to get something to eat from the dining room. You were lying on the floor with the other children; eating was never one of your favorite occupations. I was responsible for all the children, so I thought since you were taken care of, I'd check on the other two. I went down to the dining room. They were the only two people in the whole room. There were Angie and Jackie, both eating steaks, as calm as cucumbers. Although the tables were nailed down, I was amazed that the cook had bothered with them, but the Portuguese were wonderful and would do anything for the children.

When it was time for bed, the boat was lurching around. I carried you up to the room. You had your arm around my neck, and I had one arm around you, and I used the other to hold on to the ledge of the bunk. Instead of the bunk staying still, do you remember it came away from the wall? We both started yelling "help, help!" There was a journalist who had the room opposite ours. His door was open, and he was typing at the time. He came across to help. I was trying to push the bunk back, but it wouldn't go. I was pinned down by the bunk. (I do remember the terror of that.) He got it back.

CHAPTER 8

Enemy-Infested Rocky Seas

THIS IS MY earliest memory:

> We are on a boat. There is a commotion. It
> is difficult to keep my balance because the boat is
> tipping and swaying, and there are ropes strung out
> all over the place. I am separated from those I con-
> sider to be my sisters, and my mother. I am told to
> lie down on blankets, on the floor. I am clinging on
> to my shaggy lion, Leo, playing with his glass eye
> and snuggling up to his puffy, soft body, while the
> Portuguese lady reads us a story. I can hear the decks
> moaning and wailing as the wind and rain roll the
> vessel randomly, sometimes turning it in full circles.
> My tummy does not feel good. I snuggle up closer to
> my oversized friend whose familiarity comforts me,
> and whose left eye is now hanging by a thick thread.
> If all else fails, I can unzip his back and feel around
> for hidden treasures. Maybe even make myself small
> enough to crawl inside. The wind is noisily shoving
> us around, and I get a sense that the normal pattern
> of movement has been so disrupted, that the cap-
> tain is fighting to maintain the ship in an upright

position. It feels as though all intentions of moving forward have been discarded.

We are told that it is time for us to go to bed. My mother comes crazily toward me. She is zigging and zagging, and clinging on to the ropes that have been strung all about the deck for this purpose. She grabs my arm and lifts me toward her. I, in turn, cling on the front leg of my lion, lifting him along too. We bump into the narrow walls of the inner decks and make our way to our cabin. I can hear my mother wince. She lets out a little cry as she hits the walls and jerkily arrives at the doorway of the cabin. She half-drops me, and I lose my grip on Leo, but we both land on the lower bunk, and my mother lands on top of us. She pulls herself up, scoots over to the little dresser, and the entire bunk bed apparatus comes away from the wall. My mother is pinned against the wall. She screams.

The man across the hall manages to continue typing during the turbulence. The door to his cabin had opened and slammed shut throughout the storm. The door swings open. He hears the thud of furniture followed by my mother screaming and runs into our cabin. He grunts scarily as he heaves the bunks off my trapped mum.

To me, he is a hero.

It felt as though the air was spinning us around. The ship was so unsteady. I think even the officers were scared. The Portuguese are well known to be excellent sailors, said to be the best. The storm lasted a few hours. There were a few accidents—a broken leg, a broken arm, nothing as bad as it could have been. Mostly it was the crew who got hurt. We found out that they didn't use the lifeboats because the storm was so bad it would have been useless.

We knew there was a big English colony in Estoril when we docked there, and we were welcomed like celebrities. They were so surprised to see us. They told us that they didn't expect the Serpa Pinto to make it through that storm. It really was a sensational storm. It was 1943, first week in September. (During the week of September 1 through the ninth. The US Department of Commerce, Weather Bureau North Atlantic hurricane tracking chart shows storm number four reaching hurricane stage between sixty-five and sixty degrees latitude and twenty-five and forty-five degrees longitude. This would have directly intercepted the course between Philadelphia and Portugal. Hurricanes were not given names until 1952.)

On the way home, we stopped in Madeira for the day. The ship needed supplies. The poor little children were begging on the docks. Madeira was in a bad way.

You said, "Why doesn't America take care of them? They have plenty of money."

You had been ashore with Lady Howard de Walden because when we arrived, we had just passed through that dreadful storm, and we were knocked out (British for exhausted!). She had two little granddaughters of her own, and she kindly took you three children along with her own and told me you were very bright because you had said that. (My mother had told me this many, many times, but this was the first time I heard it in context with the hurricane at sea. That storm had always been referred to as a "whirlwind" because when I was little, I thought the boat was spinning.)

You kids had the run of the ship. The officers were wonderful with the children. They let Jackie use the typewriter. Jackie learned to type on that ship. The Portuguese were known to be very kind to children.

We stopped at one other smaller island first in the Azores, where they took on soldiers.

We never saw the soldiers again on the ship. I don't know where they put them, presumably the lower part of the ship. When we stopped in Madeira, we took on bananas. (I remember seeing tall, dark-skinned natives, paddling long canoes loaded with bananas. They are coming to meet the ship. I am told, "Eat a banana. This will be the last banana you will taste for a long time." What I am not told is that I would prefer dried bananas anyway. Our journey aboard ship ended in Lisbon.)

CHAPTER 9

Portugal

WHEN WE ARRIVED, there were Cooks agents telling us where we should go. We went from Lisbon to Estoril. In Estoril, you and I were booked into the Hotel Palacio, and Auntie Aylsie was sent to some sort of boardinghouse. I kicked up a fuss because we were traveling together and should remain together, so they gave us the Royal Suite at the Hotel Palacio. We stayed for six weeks. Our husbands were able to pay directly for that through Cooks. The Royal Suite was the center suite right above the entrance. It had a master bedroom, plus a room for the children. Elsie and I shared a room, and there was a sitting room.

One night, at bedtime, Angie was crying. We could tell she had a high temperature, so we asked the hotel to send for a doctor. He was Hindu, dark, black. He told us she was seriously ill. We had better take her to the hospital immediately; he thought it might be spinal meningitis. They sent me with some specimen over to the chemist. I think we had to wait until the next day for the results. He ordered an ambulance. We left you at the hotel asleep with Jackie. The three of us rode in the ambulance with Angie. It was a dark night. It was the first night of the blackout in Lisbon. The blackout stretched all along the coast, and I don't know how much further. I found out later it covered the whole of Portugal.

When we arrived at the hospital, there were big wooden gates. They opened up a little teeny part of it, and a nun looked out to see who we were. The doctor spoke to her and explained.

They put Angie in a bed. They told us to leave her, and they would look after her. We went home. The next day, I went back to pick up the result of the sample, and then we went by train to the hospital. While we were there, instead of sending us out of the room, we stood there listening to that poor child scream as they took the spinal tap. Hearing Angie scream like that has never left me. It was terrible. After that night, Angie seemed to have gained an uncanny tolerance to pain and resistance to other diseases.

What was amazing was that there wasn't a nun in that hospital who spoke English, and yet Angie managed to get anything she wanted within reason, and they could understand her. We found out that another child had come down with meningitis before Angie was diagnosed. We heard it from a cousin of the Wolfsons who lived in Portugal. Every afternoon, we would take a train to Lisbon, then a tram to the hospital. We both went because it was difficult to go by yourself. We couldn't speak Portuguese, so it helped for us to go together. By then, everybody at the hotel knew what was going on, so the English Rothschilds took it in turns to take you and Jackie out for a walk. You loved that, because you said whenever the Rothschilds took you out, they bought you ice cream. One day, when I returned to the hospital, you said "A new Japanese spy has arrived."

Little did I know until after the war, so many stories would be written about the spying that went on in Portugal. Another time, Angie said that a friend of ours had come to visit her in the hospital. He had told her that he was the secretary general of the Red Cross and was there to make arrangements for all the children from the countries at war to receive oranges. Later, I read in the paper that he was arrested for drugs.

It was during the time that Angie was in the hospital that I received a call from the ambassador's wife. She called to tell me that we were on the top of the list for people to return to England. She knew about Angie and that Angie wouldn't be well enough to travel. She understood when I said I could not leave until Angie was ready to travel too. I might be needed to help carry her or to make arrangements if we had to leave suddenly. Our pact to stay together would always be honored. All the arrangements for our return journey were made by our husbands. We received instructions by letter. You couldn't talk by phone overseas during the war.

One of the men later told me that when Angie got better and was ready to leave the hospital, the women in the hotel had banned together to object. They had all thought that she might still be contagious, so he invited her to stay at his house with his housekeeper until she got better. The housekeeper had a little girl her age. He had lived there for some time and was almost a native there, and he knew the guests and the staff in that hotel. He was a music professor at the university there. He made a reception at Rosh Hashanah for all the Jewish people around there. I think he was a bachelor, and he sent me a most beautiful basket of flowers. He said it was for the way I acted when Angie was so ill.

We couldn't understand Portuguese, so we did not have any idea if Portugal entered the war or which side it would be on. Years later, a Portuguese friend said as a child, he hid behind their refrigerator during the blackout, because he thought the planes would come from Berlin.

Angie stayed with this fellow until the last minute, until we were ready to leave. We left Portugal by plane. It looked like an army plane which had just been converted for passengers. It had some folding chairs put in. They were in rows facing the front; there were no seat belts in those days. We landed in Ireland, and I insisted you had an egg and bacon for breakfast, as we weren't likely to get that again. We'd heard of the shortages in England. You did me the favor of eating it. The plane was actually a sea plane, and it landed in the water near Sandbanks. We stepped out of it onto the wing and from there into a little boat, a row boat. It seated about twelve people. The man next to you was wearing a brand-new camel's hair coat. He had come over from America. I found that out as I apologized to him. You vomited egg and bacon all over that coat.

(Another time my mother related this. She said we had to transfer from the plane by a rope ladder that had been strung across from the plane to the rowboat. The sea was so rough that each person clung to the ropes for dear life. She said she saw one of the sailors fall overboard, but no one was steady enough to rescue him. She just told me this. I was shaken. I have had this recurring dream of crossing an narrow elevated rope bridge that is unsteady, and I have to grip and balance myself. In my dream, I never reach the waiting vehicle.)

PART 2

CHAPTER 10

Broken Glass, Broken Family, and Bombs

WE WERE WHISKED out into little private offices where a soldier stood at attention as we were questioned. I didn't think that was too welcoming.

After that, we took the train to Victoria station.

(Getting off the train is my first cohesive memory; I am looking around, and seeing what looked like a vast shell of a greenhouse. Slivers of glass remained in places but most had been broken out. For me, at five years old, my life began right there. It is where I "met" my father.)

I was wearing a beige suit under my new mink coat. I had bought the coat just before we left America, as I had to use the dollars before I came home. It was the first time not only the Jewish women were all wearing mink coats, but the Christian women were also wearing them. The spirit prevailed, "We don't know what we'll be doing tomorrow, so let's enjoy today." It came over everybody. I had bought the suit from Sylvia Morris. She was a well-known designer in England before she opened a shop on Madison Avenue. She later moved to California. She was an attractive woman with an attractive husband, but I was told her son came over to America and took all her money and spent it, and she died penniless. My friend, Vicki Harris, used to visit her in a home and found out that she never even got the presents Vicki gave her, as the help took them. Vicki took the gifts anyway, hoping that the help would be extra nice to Sylvia in return.

Your father's first words were "you can't wear that here," referring to the mink coat. I had bought it with the money we had left. You couldn't take any American money back to England, so you had to get rid of it, so what better way than with a mink coat? Jan, if this ever should be published, get some advice from a good lawyer. (Why, Mum, are you worried they'll come and get you?) No, I'm afraid they'll pull me up from the grave.

I had been told that I looked like a film star. In those days, we got dressed up all the time. I remember stepping down the steps of the train, and he was right there. (The "he" refers to my father.) He was in uniform; he was an officer in the home guard. First, he said "you can't wear that here" followed by "we're staying at the Savoy."

We stayed there for about a year. During these times you were only supposed to stay for about ten days. I don't know why but I think it had to do with spies. I think we bribed someone to be allowed to stay on. (What did you do about the bombs, Mum?) The Savoy had a basement. Before we left England, we stayed at the place behind the Cumberland Hotel, one street back from Oxford Street. We had Zelda's governess (Zelda is Mum's cousin) come and look after you, and we all went downstairs into the basement there. We could hear the guns going off in Hyde Park. You, who were five at the time, said, "Isn't Hitler silly? Doesn't he know we've got guns to shoot him down."

When we came home, there weren't so many bombs because the Germans were preparing for the buzz bombs. They weren't bombing London quite as much right after we got back.

Our rooms at the Savoy were full of lovely baskets of flowers to welcome us home, from the Bernards (my father's partner) and all kinds of people, not at all what we expected. We had a suite with two bedrooms and another separate bedroom. The three girls slept in one bedroom, and Aylsa and Nat had the adjoining room. Joe and I had the separate bedroom. We stayed at the Savoy as long as we could, but we couldn't prolong our stay any longer, so we went back to the Regent Palace Hotel, where we had stayed before we left for America.

That was another place where you let everybody know you wanted to go on the beach.

(Did you hear any bombs while you were at the Savoy?) I think we must have, but the people went on dancing. We did ballroom dancing—you know, the foxtrot, the waltz, and the jitterbug were popular then. We went down to the basement once to use it as a shelter. We didn't like it. When we first moved into the Savoy, we went into the Savoy Theatre. It was underground. We realized that wasn't very smart, because there was nothing built above it, whereas if you were in the Savoy ballroom, there were umpteen floors above. (I remember this, Mum. I remember me saying to you, "What happens if the Germans bomb us here?" And do you remember what you said?) No. (You said, "The Germans would never dare bomb the Savoy Hotel." And I felt safe.) I don't remember saying that, but I probably assumed they planned to invade England, and they'd need somewhere to stay, so they would want to stay there. On the other hand, it was right by the river Thames—an easy target, as they bombed all along the river.

One night, we were with the Cohens, and we went to a movie at the Odeon Leicester Square, and the air-raid warnings were going when we came out, so we ran as fast as we could from the cinema to the Piccadilly Hotel. We looked around and we could see all of London lit up from the bombing. We went downstairs into the basement of the hotel where there was a restaurant. We had dinner. When we were through eating, we could hear the all-clear.

One time, we sat on Peggy Goldman's roof (mum's friend) and we watched the bombing. I think they were trying to bomb St. Paul's Cathedral that night. It wasn't a clever thing for us to do. You were supposed to stay indoors when they were attacking. Sometimes we watched the planes go out and we counted them then, when they came back we counted them again to see if any were missing.

L to R Nat Cohen, Alysa Cohen, Joe Lakin, Elsie Lakin.

CHAPTER 11

Countdown for the Hit

THE FIRST BUZZ bomb that fell on London was the day we moved into Arlington House, an apartment building opposite the Ritz hotel. Joe said, "There's something strange about that bomb. It was a different sound from the others. We'll find out tomorrow what it is." The next day, they said it was a new kind of bomb. The word was that they were aiming for Buckingham Palace and, of course, Arlington House was just a stone's throw away from the palace. We used to take shelter in the hallways there because there was no glass.

You had to be careful. If a bomb was a direct hit on the building, you didn't stand a chance. If you were inside and a bomb came close by, you had to watch out for shattering glass, so the hallway was safer.

When the buzz bombs started, there was a system. When you first heard the buzz sound, you waited for it to go overhead. If you heard it really loud, and the noise stopped suddenly, that was the worst time. If it began to fade, you were safe. During the blackout, people helped one another. You didn't have to be afraid of robberies. Actually, the streets in London were safer during a blackout than they are now.

We also had to consider how to get you girls out of town. Many of the poor children were offered homes in the country away from London and, I think, other cities as well. As we discussed it, you said you wanted to go where Angie and Jackie went. Aylsa had a list of boarding schools, and she showed it to me and said, "Which one do you think?"

I said, "Battle Abbey." They made exceptions for the city children at that time.

I took you down for an interview. I think you interviewed the person who was supposed to be interviewing you. I remember you saying, "I understand it's very much like camp, do we swim every day?" You had been to camp. I think she said, "It's similar." (I was the youngest girl in that school from kindergarten until I was thirteen. Each year after my arrival, they eliminated the class I had just been in. It was a Church of England school but there was a Jewish quota— eight girls. If one graduated, another was accepted. If three graduated, then three new Jewish students were admitted. It was many years before I figured that one out.)

We had been back in England for a few weeks. The girls had to go to school, and since you wanted to be with them (I was five), we all went down to Battle. It was near Hastings. (The school was literally built by William the Conqueror in commemoration of his victory over King Harold at the Battle of Hastings. The lake, Senlac, on the estate, was named for all the blood lost during that battle. The crypt, left by Henry VIII when he abandoned the Catholic Church and tore down the monasteries, was, in later years, the main focus from my bedroom window. The tomb, to mark the place where the arrow went into King Harold's eye had equal high visibility from my window. My recurring dream is that the Germans are bombing directly at Harold's tomb, and I am crouching down beside it. For some reason it shelters me.)

We had our interview. However, right after that, the school was moved to Devonshire. We heard it was to be used as a German prisoner-of-war location. After it moved, it took seven hours to get there by train. We used to come down to visit you during the holidays. We took you to the Imperial Hotel in Devon. It had a nice beach. The hotel was on a cliff, and then we'd take you back to school to avoid the bombs. (I didn't actually go home to London until the war had ended, two years later.)

CHAPTER 12

Jan's Journey, 1945

LIKE MYSELF, MY school was also evacuated during WWII. It was moved from Sussex to the rich-soiled southern part of England, Devonshire. The outstanding feature of Killerton Park—that was the name of the house and grounds that would be my migratory residence in Devonshire—were the rhododendrons.

Killerton Park was a typical stately old English home, with rich mahogany wood interior paneling in every room, and with mature gardens that continued to flourish in their Devonshire soil, in spite of the war raging around us and inside our psyches.

Intruding into these psyches were late-night air-raid practices. Whistles would blow at random hours at night after the lights were out. This was our cue for an air-raid evacuation rehearsal. Each of the 150 girls in the school would put on their gas masks, march outdoors single file into the chilly English night air, then disappear into the foliage of the rhododendrons, which seemed to be in eternal bloom. I never doubted that the rhodos would protect me, not only from any invading German army, but also from any gases that could possibly be hurled in my direction. After crawling through the bushes, we would line up, and, immediately, the mistress would say, "All clear, girls. You may go back now," and we would file sleepily back to our dorms.

At Killerton Park, the dorms were small, only about five or six beds in each. Each of us was assigned an iron bed, under which there was a "potty." Yes, we did use the potty, but only if we had to retch, or in the middle of the night, and very rarely. There was a bowl on the dresser beside each bed. A bell was rung at six in the morning. At the sound of the ring, the matron appeared with a pitcher of water. She poured a little into our bowls, enough for us to wash our faces and clean our teeth.

Mostly, we were up long before that, but any lingerers would jump out of bed at the first sound of the bell, because the timer had started to tick, and you'd better be downstairs for prayers, or receive a demerit. We immediately went into the hall for prayers, of the Church of England variation, then breakfast, then class.

I always said my prayers before I went to sleep. I had one urgent prayer that I wanted God to hear and act upon as soon as possible.

On May 7, 1945, just after the lights had been ceremoniously turned off, the head mistress burst into our dorm. "Girls, victory. VE day has just been announced. Japan is still at war, but the war in Europe is officially over. You may get dressed and come downstairs." *Get dressed* meant full uniform, no pajamas. We grabbed our brown bloomers, beige blouses, pulled our brown tunics over our heads, and knotted our saint-inspired school ties. We jumped up, hugged each other, and ran down the stairs. I remember hugging and clinging on to teachers, matrons, all ages. We lost any notion of who we were. The youngest and oldest clinging together in a mass of relieved humanity.

British to the end, we only settled down after a final chorus of *Rule Britannia* which goes—in case you don't know—Rule, Britannia / Britannia, rule the waves (being eternally aware of our island status) / Britain never never never shall be slaves!"

* * *

The myth of our rightful school location would soon become a reality.

"Auntie" Aylsa lay among spongy white organdy pillows. According to mum, she had a cigarette in her mouth even as her body absorbed the lung and breast cancer that hungrily gnawed away her life. Angie and Jackie were sent home for the funeral. Angie told me they were going home. I asked, "Are you going because my parents are getting a divorce?" Angie promised me that wasn't why. I don't think she knew why. After Angie and Jackie had left, the matron told me it was because their mother had died.

That was when I found the best place to work out my world. You could cry in the bath and, because your body was already wet, I discovered that crying didn't make me any wetter. At the time of Auntie Aylsa's death, I hadn't really differentiated between my two mothers. I felt the loss of half a mother, though I alone knew that, and as I stared down at my already wet body, I wept for the loss, and at the same time, I wept for the exclusion.

I found out, in fact, my parents were getting a divorce.

CHAPTER 13

Battle Abbey

AFTER THE WAR, the school moved back to its place of origin—that is, back into the abbey in a tiny town called, appropriately, Battle. Battle is seven miles from Hastings in Sussex. Battle Abbey had been built by William the Conqueror in commemoration of his military victory over King Harold in 1066. The antiquity of the location added a certain awe to our prayers, which were delivered each morning in the Abbots Hall. This hall was reputed to be sixty feet long, sixty feet wide, and sixty feet high. When you looked up, it was a heady feeling, and I had to control a strong urge to faint. Four saints had their colorful banners posted on an imposing platform facing the hall, Saint Martin, Saint Patrick, Saint Mary, and Saint Etheldreda. Once you were assigned your saint, you lined up in front of said saint's banner for the rest of your school life. Mine was Saint Etheldreda. Her color was purple, and so was the tie I wore to bond me to my assignment. Myself, being Jewish, purple was about the only thing she and I had in common.

Battle Abbey gateway (as seen from the school.)

I always liked my saint. I think because nobody had ever heard of her, and my affinity there was that nobody had ever heard of me, either. She and I had one problem. As I grew older, I didn't grow taller. I found myself placed in the very front row throughout my years, and I became ever more self-conscious until, during puberty, my legs would quiver, and it was all I could do to stay upright. All the while, Saint Etheldreda watched me with her self-fulfilled smile, and no solutions to my discomfort.

In 1066, there was no central heating, and there was no central heating throughout my entire boarding school experience. The stone walls did nothing to reflect our body heat, or keep the cold damp English air on the outside, so I learned to sleep completely submerged under the blankets. We did not have fires in the fireplaces. The only place that was heated was the floor of the Abbots Hall. One awaited with anticipation the moment when "be seated" was announced. It was the one opportunity during the day that afforded our bodies a chance to give up responsibility for heat maintenance.

Prayers delivered in this atmosphere of historic religiosity were required by the entire school each day. The *King James Bible* was read from start to finish and then repeated throughout my eleven years in attendance. When I reached the age where I was required to "read the lesson," I discovered that not the entire Bible actually applied to my religion. Since the reading was rotated, and so was the lesson, the laws of chance dictate that at some point, I would be asked to read from the New Testament. Although we were in the most pious of environments, I don't recall my classmates ever having had a single discussion about the service. I have to admit, the hymns we sang will always move me. I remain steadfastly more comfortable with Church of England hymns than with "Di diyenu, di diyenu, di di-yenu, diyenu diyenu!" Somehow, William Blake's "Jerusalem the golden…on England's green and pleasant land" will always give me that fuzzy patriotic glow.

The first time I met Fanny, I was sitting on the parquet floor in the library playing jacks by myself, when I got a sense that someone was waiting their turn. Wordlessly, we began the competitive bond that endured all through our childhood. Fanny was Scottish (never say Scotch!). She was the daughter of two doctors. Her full name was Ann Francis Mary Selkirk Beaton. We were best friends and fiercely competitive. Every single morning, Fanny and I wrestled before the bell went off. I could get her to the ground only because I was fiercer, definitely not tougher. She actually weighed two stones more than me—that's twenty-eight pounds. She was remarkable to me in that at the end of each term, when we were handed our leftover rations, she ate the entire pound of prepackaged butter, followed by the one-pound bag of sugar. She ate them immediately upon receipt, and she did this time after time. Her eyes would look directly at me and sparkle with amusement. She had me there; I couldn't beat her at that.

There is something else I need to say here. For reasons that I never have understood, I was absolutely terrified to sleep in a bed by myself. I could hear sounds from the road that conjured up images of a lone motorcyclist, and though I could go off to sleep, sometime during the night, I would get spooked, and I always crawled into Fanny's bed. She never kicked me out. For the last few years, I have tried to find her to thank her. I don't even know if she is still living.

There is one other person to whom I am indebted but unable to reach. She is the classmate who managed to explain to me what the teacher had taught during my class each day. Directly after the class, she translated the lesson into words that I could understand. What I know now is that I had learning difficulties. I sat through eleven years of classes waiting for my friend to explain what the class had been about. Eventually, I was banned from going to math at all, and had to study for my GCE without schooling, except for Carol Birts. She got me through, and I passed all of my exams. GCE is the General Certificate of Education. I took my *A* Levels at sixteen. I still have perceptual differences and maize problems.

As difficult as the academic learning was, reading and memorizing were second nature. They also got me into trouble. When the lights were ceremoniously turned off by the matron on the dot of seven o'clock each night, on went my torch (flashlight), and out of the covers came Dickens, P. G. Wodehouse, sometimes even Shakespeare. There was no end to my infatuation with the English classics. After the reading marathon, there was the whispering marathon. With a dorm full of girls, there was a lot to talk about. We talked for about five years. Then I was separated out as being the ringleader. My punishment was to be placed in a dorm with older girls. It was their mission to discipline me. They set about this with enthusiasm.

Apparently, somebody in the dorm decided that I was not one of them because of my religion. This came to me as a total surprise, being oblivious to the fact that Jewish meant more than German persecution. Luckily for me, I was forewarned of a plot to destroy me by my two Irish Catholic dormmates. They had been included in the meeting. My two friends assured me that they wouldn't let anything happen to me, since they too were minorities. That was how I learned that word.

Nothing happened to me that night, but after that was Elizabeth Marchbank. I can't forget that name, though I'm told she is a most civilized woman in middle age now. However, when she was eight or nine years old, she plotted in whispered threats how to injure and victimize me. Each night, I would listen to her threats and taunts, and quake with fear and shake with anger.

One Sunday morning, we found ourselves alone in the dorm. It was the first opportunity I had had to equalize our power. We were one-on-one. I had to make her quake this one time. I took out my riding crop. She ran out of the room. I raised the crop. She hit her finger on the radiator on the way out. It bled. I never had even intended to actually strike her. I never did actually strike her, but I was reported.

My father was called, and I was summoned to Ms. Sheehan-Dare's office. She was the school principal. My father got me out of that one. He told Ms. Sheehan-Dare that since the school had raised me exclusively since I was five years old, they were solely responsible for my behavior. With that in mind, the school leadership determined that I should be confined to the attic.

Every night for two years, I climbed eight steep circular stone steps up to the tiny room in the turret. I hope you're not thinking, *That poor little kid.* I loved the attic. Nobody to whisper about me after dark. No matron listening for the slightest infraction. I still had a bed, a small dresser, and there was a narrow-paned window which overlooked the crypt where the monks had prayed and used the basement to store their wine, or so we were told.

When Henry the VIII left the Church of England, he tore down the churches, literally. All that was left was the crypt with Harold's tombstone right beside it, though rumor had it that Harold wasn't in it. He is purported to be buried at Westminster Abbey, the other victorious memorial built by the conqueror, but the tombstone is supposed to represent the spot where King Harold fell when the arrow pierced his eye. I thought of Harold quite a lot up there. I have a recurring dream of his marker. In my dream, I am crouching behind the stone. A German plane has four guns directed at me, but as they shoot in my direction, Harold's tombstone protects me every time. I wake up with my hands over my ears.

Out of my window, behind the beds of perfect blue cornflowers, was a lawn. Adjacent to the lawn, a row of pine trees lined up on either side of a walkway. I always wondered what those monks were thinking when they had to leave their lovely setting just so the king could satisfy his syphilic lust and marry Anne Boleyn, whose picture, painted by Sargent, hung alongside the big formal school staircase that was off-bounds for students.

On Guy Fawkes Night, Anne Boleyn would come out of the painting and walk around the school with her head tucked underneath her arm. I never saw her myself, but some of my friends did! Guy Fawkes Night, November the fifth, was cause for the entire village of Battle to celebrate. In front of the abbey's main gates, a huge bonfire was erected, and poor old Guy Fawkes was hung in effigy above it. After dark, the villagers carried torches. These were very long broom handle-like flame carriers, and one by one, they plunged their cargo into the bonfire, and Guy went up in flames. This set the tone for the ensuing firework celebration. No one really cared to investigate just why we were so vindictive to Mr. Fawkes. I later found out he was put to the rack and then, as though that wasn't enough, he was hung, drawn, and quartered. The year was 1605. He was thirty-five years old. His crime was his bid to defend the rights of the oppressed Catholics by attempting to blow up the Houses of Parliament. His planning left something to be desired, since he was caught in the act. I began to see why my Irish Catholic friends felt a loyalty to oppressed minorities.

So my life in the attic was quite cozy. My old dorm friends still helped me out, since I had been severed from Fanny during the initial disciplinary action. Luckily, I had no problem sleeping alone up there in the secluded sanctuary of this English boarding school so interwoven into the very foundation of English history. Though I did get spooked when I would lie in bed and it was pitch-dark and I would hear that eerie sound of the motorcycle coming down the road.

After about a year, the school deemed me fit to mingle with my peers again. I was reinstated into my old dorm, with Fanny, Carol Birts, my loyal Irish friends, Adrian and Patty, and other girls who were part of my group. The evening conversations did not miss a beat. Somehow my terror returned, and Fanny made room for me in her bed without ever waking from her sleep. We greeted each other in the morning with surprise. I never remembered climbing into her bed, and she always wondered what I was doing there. One night, she sleepwalked into my bed. I couldn't believe what was happening and yelled at her to get out. Then I just made room; that's the kind of friendship we had. My heart aches to think about it now. I regarded her as a pillar of strength who would protect me from the bogeyman; that was all it took to get me through the night. Those were the days of innocence, except when I was being punished. All eight girls spent year after year in the same dorm.

During the summer, we would run before breakfast, and when we were older, we could play tennis. Hours of lawn tennis before breakfast while we powdered the ball at each other, and developed our Segura serves for future use against each other and opposing school teams.

After a Christmas holiday one term, the Irish girls arrived late to school. There had been a terrible storm on the way over the Irish Channel. The storm was so bad and the people so seasick that when the crew asked the mayor of Dublin to move into the lifeboats, he felt too ill to go. He simply refused to leave the ship, and, shockingly, he went down with it. Then came a year when Patty did not show up at school. We learned later that she had unknowingly picked up a bomb which exploded in her hand. She suffered severe burns and lost her eye. That was my first education about the war in Ireland. She never returned to school, and I never saw her after that. I missed her.

CHAPTER 14

Divorcing Daddy/Lloyd and Solar

DURING THOSE EARLY years, after the war, I would come home for a week at Christmas, a week for Easter, and four weeks for the summer.

During my "holidays," I witnessed a different war. The warring parties were my mother and father. I do believe that the three years we lived in America sank into the recesses of my brain because of their relative tranquility. Once we returned to England, the domestic fighting raged and spewed long after the lights were turned back on in London.

Each night, my father would come home from work, stop in the hall to remove his coat, then walk straight into the living room. He would sit down at the bleached wooden mini piano, place his hands carefully on the keyboard, and play Tchaikovsky's First Piano Concerto. I can hear him now. *Da da da dah da, da dem*—those rich notes played with the loud pedal pressed to the floor. His face reflected his pleasure.

He was really good, but his family could have cared less.

"I went to tea with Sylvia today. I think she's going to leave Stanley," my mother would interrupt his rapture.

Daddy continues playing.

"Then I went to Harold to have my silver dress fitted."

Each chord played out with deliberation.

The lid of the mini piano is gently laid down.

"I have a meeting tonight."

"You were out last night. You're going to meet her, aren't you?"

'What are you talking about?"

"You think you're pulling one over on me, but you're not."

"You don't know what you're talking about."

"I have my ways of getting information. You were seen, you know."

My father would be walking toward the coat closet.

"If you keep this up, you'll be sorry."

"Get out of my way."

"You…"

"Nobody would stay with you. You talk rot, and I'm not going to listen to it."

"I'll make you pay for this."

"Oh yes, nobody else would have you. Get away, I'm leaving."

"No."

"Move."

"No."

"I'll move you, then."

"Move me and I'll fight."

And so it went. I remember the words, "My nails are long and I'll tear your eyes out."

Then I would watch my father put on his coat and leave.

We lived in an apartment building in London, 68 Arlington House. Daddy would go down in the lift, and I would watch out of the window. We were five floors up, and I could see the entrance. His car would eventually pull out of the underground garage, and I would breathe a sigh of relief. I think that relief was not because he was gone but because it meant the fighting had stopped, and no one was hurt.

One day I asked my mother, "Could you and I divorce Daddy?" I always believed that it was my suggestion that she actually followed. She did divorce him. Nat Cohen, Angie's father, acted as the intermediary. My parents were the first people I ever heard of being divorced, and it remained so throughout my childhood.

On my tenth birthday Angie informed me that the reason my parents got divorced was because my father was sleeping with "Miss Rome."

I knew Miss Rome because she was the designer at my father's business. My father had taken me to her townhouse once. I had seen a little boy there. He was in a play pen. She introduced him to me as "Lloyd." I liked Miss Rome. From the moment I was given this choice bit of information, my liking reversed itself. From that time on, I loathed Miss Rome. I didn't have to loathe her for long. Two years later, she died of uterine cancer, and she "left" Lloyd to my father! Now remember, at the time I met her, she had a husband; Lloyd had a father.

Later, she divorced the husband and managed to gain sole custody of Lloyd, whom she, with my father's consent, willed to Daddy.

Daddy asked me, "What could I say to a dying woman?"

If I'd known then what I know now, I would have answered without hesitation, "No."

So, when he was six, and I was twelve, Lloyd came to live with my father. The father who supposedly sired him, and one "uncle" would take turns taking him to soccer matches on Saturdays. When Lloyd wasn't in school, Jack (of all trades—packer for my father's business most of the time, but driver and keeper of Lloyd, as needed) was instructed to take Lloyd wherever he wanted to go, whenever he wanted to go, so Lloyd spent his childhood deciding where he wanted to go next.

Being of short attention span, Lloyd kept Jack running him from place to place. I remember watching him jump into the pool. He belly flopped in, swam to the wall, and yelled, "I want to play golf now." Out he got, dried off, and pushed on to his next moment of fancy.

Later in his life, that became a metaphor for the way he lived. He did that with women, jobs, friends, and investments. I don't know how his life will end, but he negotiates himself into a new business every two years. Somehow, he manages to find people to invest. A month ago, he called me to say that he had no food, but he had a new product. He needed money. He's fifty-six now. When he asked this time, he was crying. It is easier to refuse when he resorts to his usual way—threats, shouts, and rages. I gave him $2000. I knew I was just buying time. I found out later he was driving a 1985 Jaguar.

My mother was always gracious and kind to Lloyd. Sometimes I would bring him over for lunch, and she would say, "He's just a child. It isn't his fault." When he was no longer a child, and became insolent toward her, she changed her mind. It was easy to exclude him from family events especially since, by then, he'd moved to Hong Kong.

My father, Joe Lakin, died in London in August 14, 1965, and is buried at Bushey Jewish Cemetery. He was fifty-two. Though his doctor knew he had an aneurysm, there was nothing to be done. This was before open-heart surgery. My father refused to discuss anything about death or dying. When I was young, he would say, "You'll be an empress but you must be responsible. Leave Auntie Belle (my father's sister) in her house (owned by my father)." According to his will, his house and its contents went to his common law wife, his golf clubs went to his brother, his business to be shared between Lloyd and myself. I never heard a word about any other properties. As it turned out, his house and the beautiful antiques inside were not paid for, his business was indebted for the next decade, so the golf clubs and his Patek Philippe watch were about his only possessions. Lloyd got the watch. He just took it after my father's death.

Many years later, when my accountant asked me why I worked so hard, I remember thinking, *That was my father's inheritance.* I really got the best thing of all—a determination to work, save, maintain an intellect, and "be human." He used to say, "We're all human. Jews are just more human."

When my father died, all the stories died with him. He loved to talk about the day he allowed me to go foxhunting. I was about eleven. You had to be invited to join the hunt. We were in Newquay, Devonshire, and the riding stable there had arranged for my invitation. I found myself galloping through fields, under low overhanging trees. My horse leapt over huge logs. We scooted down narrow lanes. It felt as though we were covering half of England. If a fence was there, everyone jumped it at the same time. We bumped into each other, landed on pavement. It was a free-for-all. Anyway, I never saw the fox.

When it was over, I returned to the hotel, my adrenaline peaking. As in most English hotels, there was a lounge area where tea and alcoholic beverages were served. I sat down near the fire, anxious to tell my story. The way my father described it, one by one, the people nearest me would move away. He said he looked up and he noticed the room was empty. It was the smell, or, rather, stench, of me. It drove the hotel guests away, and apparently, the lobby wasn't far enough. Daddy said he could hear them starting up their cars. I do remember a caterpillar crawling out of my hair that night.

The way my father trained me to work was pretty simplistic; in a word, bribery. We were at Selsdon Park Hotel in Croyden when I was given my first riding lesson. No sooner was I up there, astride a little bay pony, when I knew this was the ultimate joy. Being raised up and viewing the world from this altitude, having the equivalent of a car to steer, even if there was a fierce battle between moving forward and preventing the steering wheel from grabbing grass along the way, and, of course, the vehicle was surely the most perfect creature on earth. I was smitten. My father had his bargaining tool.

I was six years old. He told me if I would be top of my class every year until I was twelve, I could have the best prize of my life. I heard "if you are top of your class, you can have a horse." That year, I was top of the class. I got a radio.

CHAPTER 15

She Paws the Earth and Rejoices in Her Strength

Solar and Janice

SOLAR WAS PURE Arab. With perfect formation, her long blond mane was offset by a rich chestnut body. Her aristocratic looks were suited to her perfect bloodline which, unfortunately for me, conformed to her skittish personality. This horse could move, and she could jump. Sometimes that meant over real jumps, but often it meant a shy; shying is when a startled horse jumps sideways. She shied at trees, she shied at noise, she shied at cars, and especially, she shied at jumps. She gave some warning. The hairs on the top of her pointed ears would almost touch, but there wasn't always time to heed the warning.

Solar was stabled at Beaufort Park Hotel, the riding school near the Abbey. She had been mine for three weeks when we were out with a group and decided to play "fox and hounds." I was to be fox. I don't remember much of that day. I do remember seeing Solar's ears touch and a tree looming close. That wasn't the tree I went into. I was prepared for that one, but not the one opposite it. It is said that horses can always find their stable. In this case, Solar wasted no time in heading for home. She arrived riderless and notably delighted.

Sometime later, I fumbled my way there and then collapsed. Heaven knows how. Later, I was told there was blood running all down my face. Much later, I discovered my ear was torn up, and my front tooth was missing. Some of the top teeth were loose, and the bottom ones were chipped.

I woke up with my head unsupported over the backside of a wooden chair, and my head, neck, and shoulders hurt like the dickens. I had no recall of the actual fall or how I got back to the stable, and I don't to this day. All I remember were Solar's ears getting dangerously close and a tree trunk looming toward us.

My problem was that I was to be in "detention" that Saturday. I had so many conduct marks that my punishment was to last for three hours. The matron, Mrs. Stancomb, known by our dorm as Shaky, or Stinky Stancomb, had prowled the dark halls at night and managed, once more, to catch me talking after lights-out. What was worse was I hadn't stopped after the first or second time. She sought vengeance. I had disobeyed the rules three times in a row. The price was three hours detention.

Shaky was the first person to see me after the ambulance delivered me back to school. I had been left in a contorted semiseated position on the bench in the Abbots Hall, unable to support my head with my neck, so my body was keeled over to one side. She walked over full of sympathy. In my barely lucid state, I was mentally chuckling to myself that I had won. X-rays revealed a crack in my skull. I was in bed for a month. Someone had thoughtfully covered all the mirrors in the sanatorium, so the scabs on my face had dropped off when I finally assessed the damage. My upper left front tooth haunted my otherwise decent looks for the next twenty years. The other teeth did tighten back up, and thanks to the new release of penicillin, one shot each day for a week sped up the healing of my face and ear.

America had become my mother's home away from home since the divorce. I had about five fountain pens shaped like Mum's favorite mode of crossing the Atlantic, the cruise ship *Queen Elizabeth the second*, better known as QE2.

Mum's quest for a husband was foremost for both of us, so it was my father who saw me before I had seen myself after my "accident." His face reflected something I couldn't quite read. He later told me it was horror, but that he had been forewarned.

Three months later, I mounted Solar again. I had been humbled.

Once, while riding in the row in Hyde Park, Solar stopped short, and I was tossed off right in front of a policeman. I was so paranoid of Solar galloping loose through the park and across Bayswater Road, a scarily busy street running parallel to the park, that I had a dead man's grip on the reins. To my utter amazement, I did a complete flip and landed on my feet right in front of the bobby. We both stood face-to-face. I didn't say a word; neither did he. With reigns still in hand, I grabbed the saddle, mounted Solar, waved goodbye as if this was routine.

I moved Solar from the center of London to a stable near Richmond Park.

Deer roamed free in Richmond Park. Now and then, Solar, through brush, gorse bushes, brambles, nettles, and wild flowers, would catch a glimpse of deer eyes. She would sound out her acknowledgement and resume snatching at passing edibles.

Solar and I spent endless hours practicing dressage, jumping over logs, and crossing the winding river sometimes mounted, other times wading through a not-so-gentle current. I would coax my reluctant, snorting companion to take another step until, to my relief, she would clamber up the bank on the other side. Then we would wander through the park peacefully, with Solar whinnying anytime she sensed another horse might be within earshot.

One day as I stepped off the bus and my foot hit the ground, I heard a whinny. It was my girl. She did it that day, and she did it every time I arrived after that. That was the moment I knew that Solar and I had bonded.

She was mine until I gave her to my friend who had always adored her. I left for America. She was dead within a month. My friend had to leave town for a few days and had left someone to look out for Solar. She returned to find out that Solar had died in the field where she had been grazing. Her corpse was immediately sent to a glue factory. My friend filed a lawsuit against the "caregiver" and tried to apologize to me. My heart ached for the indignity.

PART 3

CHAPTER 16

America

IT WAS DECEMBER 1957. With grandma's voice imploring me, "Please, Janice, here, have this cup-a tea before you leave," I mounted the steps and boarded the plane to America.

My first impression was how light and shiny America is. The impact was intense and immediate. I was bombarded by images of elongated colorful cars, so exaggerated with their outstretched shiny fins, and fenders. I felt as though I was part of a movie set. It took thirteen hours to cross the Atlantic, the plane was a DC 6 with passenger accommodation of twenty-five seats, plus fourteen sleepers. The ticket was for a sleeper, a bunk-style bed, which was opened up by the steward after dinner had been served, and the cabin lights were lowered. All I knew about America was the words to *Oklahoma*, *Annie Get Your Gun*, cowboys, and Danny Kaye movies, and that my mother had told me all my life that you could get all kinds of cereals in little boxes.

My geography lessons at Battle barely touched on any history since the Boston Tea Party. The Revolutionary War and the Civil War were completely omitted from my history lessons. I was too busy learning about Oliver Cromwell, the bastard, literally, and Lord Nelson, the hero.

I was enamored with the American accent. The movie *Giant*, with Elizabeth Taylor and James Dean, was playing, and Texas played a glamorous role in my imagination. There was a glitch in my non-existent career goal which had to do with the English versus the American educational systems, and my visa which did not permit me to get a job. School was over for me at sixteen. I now felt empowered to educate myself. I set about it by conferring with the local librarian. I was told there were American classics. Had I read them? American classics? Nobody ever mentioned that before. It almost seemed an oxymoron. Though I loved the accent, it did after all have a slight twang of slang. Boarding school was thoroughly *Oliver Twist* and "Ode to a Grecian Urn." However, *The Scarlet Letter* and *A Place in the Sun* led the way to a more grounded look at my adopted country.

The colorful cars and creative commercials did not distract me from my bent of homesickness. England's "green and pleasant lands" began to haunt my psyche. After three weeks of living in New York with my mother and stepfather, Fred Kahn entered my life in the form of a blind date. My mother warned me, "He likes sports, so if you like him, pretend you like sports."

Our first and blindest date was to a basketball game. His college team, University of North Carolina, was undefeated, a term I had never heard applied to sports before. The team was to play at Madison Square Garden, and that was the invitation. I went. This was the first blind date I'd had where the setup person had actually said, "He's a nice guy" and not "He drives a (fill in the blank) fancy car" or "He goes to (fill in the blank fancy) college." None of which meant a hill of beans to me.

CHAPTER 17

Married

HE WAS FROM Asheville, North Carolina. I had visited him at his father and stepmother's home one time. He had described the home as a cabin.

I thought of a cabin as small, more like a "Hansel and Gretel" cottage but without the quaint charm. I was unfamiliar with the wormy chestnut, woodsy, spacious, guns-on-the-wall style. This mountaintop cabin was four thousand square feet of luxury.

But Fred had blue eyes, dark hair, a slurry accent, and an honest face, and he was tall like all Americans. That was all I needed to commit myself to the one thing my father had warned me about. "You think you'll like suburbia, Jane (my father's nickname for me), but you won't. You'll hate it," Daddy had whispered after my honeymoon.

I had to find out what the "it" was that I would hate. Asheville was part of the Southern Bible Belt. This didn't faze me. The liquor laws that disallowed individual drinks to be bought at bars, yet permitted whole bottles of booze to be brought into the bar, and consumed by the guests meant little to my naive spirit. What it actually meant was that Southerners became accustomed to leaving the bar with just a receipt in their hand. Liquor took on a whole new meaning. And I became educated in listening to the sweet sounds of vomiting after a particularly celebratory evening. And I was pregnant.

I wondered if I would give birth to one huge tomato. All I wanted to eat were canned tomatoes. I'd never particularly liked them before or since, but Stuart was surely made of them. Later, he became allergic to all foods containing red. Tomatoes, strawberries, and derivatives caused massive breakouts. Any rate, he was born three weeks earlier than expected on January 21, 1959, in the late hours of the day. The doctor put me out of my misery with twilight sleep, none too soon from my perspective.

Later, they brought in the black-footed, black-handed infant. I remember looking out of the hospital window. The night was dark and clear, and I could make out the stars. It was one of very few moments in my life when I consciously made a note to remember. I looked into that sky, prolonging the pleasure. I rejoiced. I knew in my heart that at that very moment, my life was fulfilled. I had given birth to a son. It turned out that the black hands and feet were due to the ink used for identification purposes.

The child, we named him Stuart, grew. The marriage shrunk. Another baby came along. We were delighted. This time a daughter, Lauren. Perfect. I was ready for more when Freddy wondered out loud, "What else is there to have? We've got one of each?" That worked. But my cup didn't runneth over. I stayed at home and spent the next eight years lonely and disillusioned about motherhood. Apparently, my fantasy mate saw his role of husband quite differently from my expectations.

Fred went to work for his father. For $7,500 a year, he rose at five in the morning and returned home at eight in the evening. He did the buying, selling, and organizing in the hide business, and he oversaw the dying and inventorying in the rag business. His was the type of personality that, after twenty years of this, when the business was sold, he could account for the mountains of rags to the last dollar and, since he was an inherently clean person, the smell of hides became a moot point. He did tell a story. One day, while stacking the hides, he noticed a tail on the one at the bottom of the stack. He pulled at it to remove the hide from the pile, but the tail disassociated itself from the hide, and he went flying to the back of the plant, tail in hand.

On our wedding day, when the rabbi said "you may kiss the bride," with my face open and awaiting a kiss, my brand-new knight deliberately knocked into me. I went staggering around on the pulpit. My heart hiccupped. I think now that his life, of mostly male influences, and my life, around females does not help our compatibility. I was nineteen and he was twenty-four when we married. I was to learn to live with a man whose tantrums were often to do with food; who believed that keeping warm in bed meant tucking the blankets in on both sides of himself; who spent weekends away from home, coming home at night, though. My job was to care for the babies I listened to an ongoing critique of my nonhousekeeping, noncooking skills, I even lacked the talent to find my own happiness. I went to sleep. I slept for about three years. I was awake long enough to fix breakfast and get the kids to play school, then pick them up, fix dinner, and go back to sleep. In the kitchen, I wept.

CHAPTER 18

The Green Circle

TO ADJUST TO culture, country, and pending motherhood, I decided to read the "American" classics. In spite of my A Levels in English Literature and Language, we studied only English classics, so I asked at our local library if there was such a thing as "American classics." The librarian was astonished but delighted at my ignorance. That night, I dreamt that the librarian was, in fact, Shakespeare. So Shakespeare knew me and asked me, "What are you doing here?" And I woke up! Another night I dreamt that I was "hog-tied," like a line of sausages, hands to feet, repeat,…to myself.

It was the early '70s. I heard that the exclusive ladies charitable club, the Junior League, was hosting a luncheon, the normally segregated, "no Blacks, no Jews" policy was temporarily suspended. The club was looking for volunteers to be trained to go into the first-grade classrooms in the Asheville schools to teach about "the Green Circle," a program designed especially for children to learn how to appreciate each person for themselves. While there, we were to interact with the teachers to learn their reactions to integration.

We filed into lunch and seated ourselves. The sound of ladies' chatter made me wonder what I was thinking being there, when I noticed the lady on my right had an unusually melodic gentle voice, a wonderful tan, and blue eyes. I must have trusted her, because I told her I wanted to volunteer for this program particularly because

I am Jewish. She gave me a mysterious smile at that. Her name was Lavie Michaels. She was so unusual that I described her to Freddy when I got home. He said, "She's Black."

I said, "How do you know?"

He answered, "I know."

Lavie was my entrance into a new awareness of our hometown. She and her husband, an internist, were looking for a home in our neighborhood, so I decided I was going to find it for them! By the realtor's lack of enthusiasm, I soon realized something was off-kilter here. I wasn't sure if it was me being Jewish or Lavie being Black. Happily, the Michaels family did find a house, and we were invited to their first party. It was a blast. Everybody seemed to know us. We were the only White faces there.

We coordinated our schedules to work the Green Circle together. We listened to the concerns of Black mothers, that their children were to be sent to the "White" schools. They feared their five- or six-years-olds would be spending their school days in unfamiliar neighborhoods, far away from their homes.

Lavie was the first person who tried to explain the Muslim connection to the Black culture to me. Our children attended the same school. Their son, Otis, took Lauren to her senior prom and attended Stuart's wedding.

When I was twenty-five, the University of North Carolina in Asheville had offered a seminar for women to discover their job capabilities. We checked the questions off with a pointed pencil and were scored according to where the points had broken through to the back side of the paper. I was the only one who scored inconclusive. They couldn't figure out whether I should work with people or alone, or what sort of work.

Community Life

SECTION C   SUN., MARCH 22, 1970

Green Circle;

How It Grows

Mrs. Fred Kahn presents the Green
Circle program to an enthusiastic class at
Newton Elementary School. Mrs. E. Al-
fred Kramer and Mrs. John E. Shackle-

volunteers are
Mrs. H. M. Bo
Mrs. Roy W.
lany, Mrs. R

It was through this test that I learned that I would probably live to be at least seventy-five. It was that knowledge that changed my life. Inconclusive, perhaps that was an advantage in that I was versatile, or was it that I simply didn't fit anywhere? I had read a book as a teenager. It was called *The Egg and I* by Betty McDonald. It was the story of a young woman with no skills, but she just believed she could learn on the job.

In those days, I was acutely aware of commercials, both TV and radio. They were new to me and very American. I thought I could do better than what I was hearing on radio. I decided to write my own. I chose a couple of familiar dress shops and a restaurant, and I wrote.

I used my little tape recorder to voice them. I then visited the businesses, played the spots, and sold them. The fact that they were not formatted at all, and they ran all kinds of different lengths, didn't seem to faze anyone. Next thing I knew, my voice was heard over all the radio stations. The problem was, I couldn't make a living. I applied for a job at WISE Radio. I got it. I called them back and said I had lied on my resume. I hadn't. I was told, "I don't care. Come in on Monday."

I said, "I can't."

I was told, "You will." I was ecstatic and terrified.

I got the job and saw a psychiatrist for marriage counseling. Freddy and I both went. I don't know how the shrink explained me to Freddy, but by using analogies, he changed my perspective of my husband. He also changed my perspective of myself. When I told him, "Freddy wouldn't let me," he said, "Oh, really, how did he stop you?" I knew I was the answer. He wasn't. I was stopping myself.

London and Asheville were not as far apart as I thought! Freddy saw me differently from anyone I had ever met. He didn't take me seriously! I took myself very seriously. Sometimes when, deep in thought, I would walk toward something important, totally focused, like the laundry, the refrigerator, the back door. I would get a sense I wasn't alone, or was I? Then, I'd realize he was walking in precision, tiny-for-him steps behind me. He had it down to such a fine art that when I came out of my reverie, I'd marvel at his skill and love the slapstick humor. We had our own understanding of allowable rough and tumble, like out of the blue, he would pick me up and playfully carry me a couple of steps on his shoulder, putting me down as I clung on to him for dear life. This was a routine when he returned from a trip. I had had a stiff neck for a few days and was taking ibuprofen and walking around with my head stuck to my left shoulder when he came bursting through the kitchen and swooped me up while I yelled, "Nah…I've got a stiff ne—" Too late. My head hit the ceiling. I saw stars, literally. When my feet touched the ground, I finished, "neck, stiff neck. No. No, wait a minute. It's gone!" And it never came back.

On another appointment with the counselor, I mentioned that WISE was changing my job from mornings to afternoons, which meant I couldn't pick my children up from school. He said, "Do they value your work?"

"I think so."

"Then tell them you can't change and see what happens." I felt empowered. The next day when I followed that suggestion and the only response was "aha, okay."

Those were the days before the corporate structure had hit radio stations. I would sit in my office hacking away at the typewriter while my boxer sat beside me. His water bowl in the corner, people would come and go while he drooled and farted his way to their hearts.

One day, a rep brought a black snake into the office. I had been warned by the receptionist at the front desk that it was on its way. Bob Rogers thought that I, being a big city girl, would be intimidated, so he hid the snake in a shoebox. He walked into my office, popped the lid off, and I immediately put my hand in to stroke the scaly critter. It felt better than it looked. This encouraged Bob, so he allowed the snake to uncoil itself and slither around my office. I went on typing. Bob left the office. I watched the snake. It hid for cover. The next day, some kind person brought in a live mouse for the snake. I left while the snake dined.

Then I went to London for a week. When I returned, Rick Jorgensen, the owner of the station, confessed to me that the snake had not been seen since I left. I said, "I know where it is."

"How?"

"Watch this." I went straight to a piece of carpeting that was rolled up in my office. "It's inside there." Rick called for some help. Three deejays came in to unfold the heavy rug. They uncovered my new office mate lying there curled up and satisfied. It stayed with me for months. We were fine as long as it wasn't feeding time.

In spite of my own immaturity, my children grew. I had a recurring dream about Lauren. I am standing in a river. The river is rising rapidly. My legs are buckling from the undertow. Two things happen. The river separates us, and I struggle to reach her, waking up before I do. Or I hold her above the current until my arms can't stand it, and I wake up with my arms stretched above my head and my shoulders aching as I put them down. I know now why I worried about Lauren, but that comes later.

The radio station was a seething hive of emotions. Paul Liddy, the office manager, ruled all paper. Paper was my nemesis. It controlled me. The system required that orders be turned in to Liddy to be processed, one copy to be filed by sales rep, one copy to go to accounting, and one copy to go to the copy department. My desk doubled as filing system, reference system, planning system, drop-off for tapes, notes, letters, photos. Each item became subject to the later objects, until the pile became barely recognizable as business-related. I could lay my hands instantly on anything I needed. One day, Liddy decided to teach me neatness. Using his arm as a broom, he swept my desk directly into the trash. He picked the day that Lauren was to have her wisdom teeth removed, and Freddy was to have hernia surgery. I ran at Liddy screaming. I jumped at and on him. By today's standards, I assaulted him.

"Where's my desk?"

"In the trash can." I hadn't thought of the trash can. I cried with relief.

He apologized saying, "I didn't know you cared, Jan."

CHAPTER 19

Radio Bedlam versus London Culture

I ONLY EVER met one deejay whose ego underestimated his ability. His name was Bruce Bisson, and he did get a job in NYC. Most disc jockeys were (often) so voice-enamored they lost tap of their surroundings.

To get into the control room, the deejays had to walk through the office. This allowed Liddy to use his eternal New Jersey wit to needle them as he felt the urge. One of the best-looking guys had the worst disposition. Rumor had it that he carried a gun.

Then it happened. He took offense at one of Liddy's remarks. He grabbed Liddy's head, pulled it down on the desk, and pointed the gun. He pointed it, but by then he had an audience. He became distracted as they gasped. True story. Grappling with Liddy was so utterly out of context. Other than Rick, he was the only organized person in the place. Even his hair was slicked down and controlled. He was a city boy. Then this kid—handsome, rugged, and deep voiced—decides to tackle him, gun in hand. This was a long way from the life I had imagined.

My father's showroom in London was brimming with fashion. Racks of dresses in one area, suits in another, and coats in another. My father, always handsome and dapper, five-foot-one, immaculately dressed in his Savile Row tailored suit, began his business day by ceremonially walking through the showroom, wishing each person "good morning." He would sit behind his desk long enough to glance at the headlines of the *Daily Express*, then he walked between the racks of new stock, greeting staff in passing, and ceremonially left the building to meet his friends for coffee.

When the Suez Sinai War broke out in 1956, my father said to me, "I'm going to have to close the business until this is over."

"Why?"

"They've all signed up to fight."

"For who?" England, Israel, and France were all on the same team.

"For Israel." We all felt, as English as can be, these Jewish Englishmen had fought for England in WWII. Now they were fearful that Israel would cease to exist without them. The conflict was fought and over in one week and two days. After the fighting had started, political pressure from the United States and USSR forced Israel, France, and the United Kingdom to withdraw.

My father's business address was 32 Great Titchfield Street. Daddy would leave me sitting in his car on Friday nights before going to Grandma's for Shabbat. The hub of groceries being delivered, along with racks of ladies' clothing and pushcarts, all vying for space to move their wares, gave the area a particular London-Jewish neighborhood appeal.

It was December of that year that I boarded the BOAC plane for America.

But my father was dead and London a memory.

It was time for the annual WISE Christmas party. The station owned a ski lodge in Wolfe Laurel. We were invited to go up there and spend the night and ski the next day. A boom box on the mantel kept everyone in touch with the station. In 1985, when Rick stood on a chair to make an announcement, there were great shouts of "hush, the *führer* wishes to speak." Spontaneously, everyone, except me, did the nazi salute and chanted "heil." This was intended as the greatest sign we could give him to show our appreciation and affection. I felt the emotions that they all felt, but I was a different generation, a different culture. In this moment of expectation and delight, the nazi salute didn't cut it for me.

Standing on the chair, Rick announced that he, along with others, had purchased the FM radio signal. Now we would cover eighty counties instead of three. The conflicts among us would reach a whole new level.

I had heard that the FM signal was for sale and had mentioned the rumor to him, stating in the same breath that I was ready for the job of sales manager.

One did not look at Rick directly to converse. He continued to work at the computer throughout most conversations. It became second nature to talk to the screen as though it was making the decision. He grinned when I told him the news. I had the feeling it wasn't news to him. He said we'd talk about it in three weeks. Throughout those weeks, I kept waking in the night, gripped with panic. I decided to list the reasons I should have the job and beside that, the reasons I should not. Should not won. When we met, I came to him with my lists. He said he wasn't interested, that he'd decided I should have the job. His reason was, since he was taking a huge risk, I should be willing to take a risk, especially since I never had. I explained that I didn't understand ionosphere (a layer in the atmosphere that effects the signal). Neither did I have a clue about microwave, frequency adjustments, directional antennae; in other words, after twelve years in radio, I didn't speak the lingo. He said that was totally irrelevant; nobody else did, either! I wasn't about to undo his plan.

Since Rick's voice was somewhat monotone with an almost electronic pitch, whenever we quoted our boss, we spoke to each other as robots. After Rick sold the station, the new owner was appalled when he interviewed each of us in front of each other. As we quoted Rick, we automatically reverted to a nasal mechanical speech. He didn't understand that we had had the freedom to do this openly, and it was not intended as an insult.

By then, we could all mimic our new boss, and it was intended as an insult! Lips down, chest out, hands raised into fist, thumbs pointing toward chest, "Er...that's not the way we did it in Tupelo."

The day the bankers were coming to finalize the deal, Rick had come to work all dressed up in a designer suit. We were all awed by his appearance—six feet, six inches of him in his Sunday best. I knocked on his door, and when I opened it, there he sat, his face all covered with Chiquita banana stickers.

"Rick, you can't do that."

"Why not?"

"You've got the bankers coming in a few minutes."

"Oh," he said, and got on the floor on all fours and lifted his leg against his desk. Remember, Rick did not drink or take drugs. His eccentricities broke the tension and were part of his genius. He managed us with total leniency and tolerance, but his long hours and our paychecks reinforced our reliance on his guidance.

One day, he explained to me that he never wanted to be considered any different from any other member of the staff. He told me then that my salary was actually larger than his. When the station sold for $6,500,000, he sent me a card. He had written: "Roses are reddish, violets are bluish, I got the money and you didn't!" He deserved the money, and I didn't!

From Rick, I learned to make sure that if an employee was being accused of wrongdoing, the accuser always related the story in front of the person accused. I learned to put facts in chronological order and to document them. I learned that presentation was key to product development, but the product had to be top-quality to flourish. I learned not to judge by instinct but to let patience and tolerance always have a major role in the judgment.

A receptionist sat in the entrance lobby. It was more usual to call on clients at their offices, but they had to come to the station occasionally. There were five cats that belonged to the station. Usually, one cat sat in the in-box on the lobby desk, another in each guest chair; sometimes, two to a chair. One day, a car dealer was doing business in the sales office when a mouse ran through. He jumped out of the way, avoiding the mouse and the three cats following in hot pursuit. The mouse couldn't find its way out of the office. I remember asking my client to hold on the phone while I grabbed a couple of cats so the mouse could escape. Another rep had a hold of the cats, while another one herded the mouse out the front door. We immediately returned to business without comment. Thankfully, the client continued to spend his money.

There were times when Rick would enter the lobby, his face distorted by a twisted Kleenex protruding from each nostril, rhinoceros-style. We'd just say, "Hi, Rick," and it was business as usual. His curly Viking hair and six-foot-six towering presence allowed his eccentricities to blend with his personality.

When Rick bought the WISE AM radio signal on August 1 of 1970, he was twenty-three, a business school graduate. In 1984, he purchased WLOS-FM. He raised the money to buy WLOS-FM by giving up 50 percent of his business to several partners. Instead of having 100 percent of WISE-AM, he had 50 percent of WISE-AM and WLOS-FM, which was worth considerably more. On December 31, 1986, he sold the AM and FM stations. In 1989, Rick explained to me that due to changes in the capital gains tax law (at that time the capital gains tax rate was 20 percent) which took effect on January 1, 1987, he and his partners were ready to sell both stations. They wanted $6,000,000."

After my shock, I must have had an epiphany, because I figured that if every available commercial was sold, the value of commercials sold under the current rate card would not come close to the formula Rick handed to me.

I picked a few brains, mostly Fred's, and we made it happen. The station sold for $6,500,000, and ten months later, I was out of a job.

I had worked for Rick for seventeen years.

CHAPTER 20

Why, Jackie, Why?

MY MOTHER LIVED through two world wars. When she was six years old, they were living at Gunton Road in London. Her mother, my grandma, had her newborn infant, Beatrice, in her arms when a neighbor came to the door. The neighbor pointed across the hill where a German dirigible had landed. I asked Mum, "What did you do then?" She said before she had a chance to see it, my grandma grabbed her arm to pull her back into the house, then immediately shut the door and closed the curtains. At ninety-one, she still remembers that.

The morning my mother tried to explain to me that Angie and Jackie were not my sisters still resonates with me. It was very soon after we returned to England in 1943 after being inseparable for the three years of our evacuation. I was five, Angie was seven, and Jackie was ten. My mother was trying to explain to me that it was time for us to go to school; that means different schools.

According to our ages, I should have been closer to Jackie's younger sister, Angie, but it was Jackie whom I adored.

Jackie and Janice

I loved her easy laugh, I loved her teasing way with me, I watched and admired her and tried to mimic her. I can see her now: It is 1948. The music is playing loudly. We are dancing in the living room of her father's flat at 19 Fursecroft, George Street in London. The living room has beige carpet. Jackie is laughing and shaking her blond head to the music. She encourages me to act silly. It is late afternoon. We are both pretending to be sophisticated grown-ups. The only strong color in the room is Jackie's blond hair and her bright red "Marilyn Monroe" lipstick. The gramophone is black with a Chinese design painted on it. The music is Latin American, and I have one arm raised in the air in front of me and the other hand on my hips which were moving as close to the beat of the music as my body knew how.

"Ha-ha-ha," she laughs and claps her hands. "Someday you will be famous, Janice. You'll see, you bad little thing. Here now, it's time to go home and show your mummy how you learned to dance. Ha-ha." I never understood what was so funny. I felt like a performing chimp, but I would have gone all night if she would let me. Her vivacity was contagious, and when she was having fun, it was impossible not to join her.

"Jackie, will you come and be famous with me?"

"No, sweetie, I don't think so." Suddenly the mood changed, and Jackie's face became strangely serious.

Since we were five years apart, Jackie matriculated and left school before me. I still spent every moment I could in their flat during the school breaks. A couple of years later, as I am entering puberty, I reach a new level of admiration. Each visit is rare now and memorable. Our age difference has become more significant. I am still a kid, but to me, Jackie is an adult. I pay closer attention to details. It is as though I could feel her separating from her past. I want to remember her singing a calypso song in her sweet high-pitched voice like a sensuous night club singer, "Rum and Coke Coke Cola…Rum and Coke Coke Cola," hips swaying, shoulders shimmying, as she opens the sliding door of the wardrobe and pulls out the full-length white mink coat her father had given her for her sixteenth birthday. Still in her nightie, she sensuously puts one arm into the sleeve, then the other, wrapping herself cozily into the luxurious fur. She doesn't miss a beat as she stares at herself in the mirror, humming her Latin song. As she hums, now and then she exaggeratedly takes a fake drag from the unlit Players cigarette, which dangles from an elegant cigarette holder. Occasionally she remembers to blow out an imaginary cigarette puff while she hums and sings to the music. "Rum and Coke, Coke Cola, Rum and Coke Coke Cola. Jan…" Never letting her eye wander from the image of herself in the mirror, she calls me to share her admiration for herself.

"You're okay," I say. "But bloody learn the rest of the words."

"Janice, nobody cares about the words as long as you move to the music. Look!"

She shapes her lips for a fake puff of smoke exhalation as she holds the unlit cigarette away from the coat and goes off doing a conga step. One, two, three, kick.

"Rum and Coke Coke Cola, Rum and…," the white mink coat dragging the floor behind her.

The brown boarding school uniform of her boarding school days has long gone. Jackie morphed out of childhood when she married Bert. The struggle to excel in sports and academically is all behind her. Her self-appointed task now is to prove to her father that she can be the woman his movies depict. She is a diminutive five-foot bride; the groom is over six feet. She is seventeen; he is thirty-three. Angie and I are bridesmaids.

It is her wedding day. She wears a white lace bridal gown. Her white platform shoes belie her petite build. Today the new image has begun. She will be a tall, shapely blond. There will be no more learning the new dances with girly partners, no more singing along with hit records, no more walking in crocodile style (two by two, as in school) down village streets.

As each guest is formally announced, she holds out a limp gloved hand, allows her lips to curl at each side momentarily, and immediately attends to the next guest in line. She is now a robotic beauty bending and reaching on cue. Almost all signs of animation have disappeared. She seems unaware of her husband standing beside her. The blue eyes are brighter than usual, but all emotions are hidden behind a blank stare. Today the twinkle is gone. The mischievous mouth is sullen. There is music, but when Jackie dances, she stares straight ahead. She has the appearance of a mechanical doll.

"Why are you marrying Bert?" I had asked.

"I just want to get married," she had answered.

I shook her hand and searched her face for signs of life. Her eyes deliberately averted mine. Later, I decided I would try to talk to her.

It would be years later, but I didn't know that then. I didn't know about her illness either.

Ten years pass. I knew that Jackie had a daughter a while back. She would be about eight now. I am married myself.

I have managed to get in a quick trip to England to visit my father and attempt to look up the remnants of my childhood culture. Jackie is living in a sleek apartment building on Sloan Square. I walk into the marble lobby and, as is the norm in London, I open the elevator gate and press number two. The door is opened by a slender young woman. She is holding a little girl by the hand.

"Mrs. Shalet, please?" I ask. To the child I say, "What is your name?"

"I'm Caroline. Are you from America?"

"Yes, sweetie. I was a friend of your mum and Auntie Angie when we were children. I was a bridesmaid at your mummy and daddy's wedding.

"Oh, I know which one you are in the picture."

"And, Caroline, my mummy was your grandma and grandpa Nat's maid of honor.

"Oh!" She turns to the young woman.

"This is Pia. She's our au pair." Caroline's voice is almost husky, almost scratchy, yet charmingly childlike and unusually memorable.

"Hello, Pia."

"Right dis way." I notice a slight accent as Pia leads me down a plush carpeted passageway. The door to the bedroom is open. I pick up the black bra and stockings. Each had been dropped on the floor as she made her way to the bed. I don't know if she has any clothes on. She takes a delicate puff of her cigarette and blows three perfect smoke rings as she reclines against a mass of pillows. The phone is up against her ear. She motions me to sit on the edge of her bed. She cocks her head to one side, lips in pout mode. I think she is about to assess me.

"Janice, my darling, you look nice." She nods in my direction while holding the phone with one hand and covering it with the other.

"Thank you, and you look okay yourself for an old bird!" I retort. Jackie chuckles and returns her attention to the phone call.

"And would you send four braised lamb chops, pureed spinach, and a mousse aux marrons entiers. Thank you so very much, Francois. The "the-ank you so very m'uch" said in the world's thickest snob English. Our beautiful English education came in handy at times like this. Jackie hangs up the phone.

Always one to relish sensationalism, Jackie immediately got to her subject.

"Did you hear I tried to commit suicide?" she says with a curious half smile.

"Yes, as a matter of fact, I did," I reply. "I really don't think that's something to be proud of. In fact, I think it's selfish. You have a young child."

"Jan, it was an accident, actually," she wheedled. "I couldn't sleep and forgot how many sleeping pills I'd taken."

"Okay," I said, "but be more careful next time."

Jackie was more careful the next time.

I'm back home in Asheville when I get the call.

"Hello, Jan, it's Angie. A long silence. "Jackie died last night. I thought you ought to know." I can hardly hear her.

"You know she had lymphoma."

"Yes, Ange."

"But that's not why she died."

There was an inquest. Suicide by overdose of barbiturates was the ruling. Her blood work showed no signs of lymphoma.

Over the years, Angie has tried to help me piece together how it happened.

The day, like many others, Jackie tells Pia she's going to rest for a while and to wake her after an hour. After two hours, Pia takes a cup of tea into Jackie. Pia taps her softly on the shoulder. Pia tries to raise Jackie to a sitting position. Jackie just flops to one side, her head lolling around without control. Pia becomes frightened and calls Bert.

"Jackie, I tink she took doz tablets again." Her voice is shaking.

"Count how many are left and tell me."

"None are left."

"Pia, call an ambulance and I'll come straight home."

It is a typically overcast day in London. Bert walks home. Nobody knows why he didn't drive or take a taxi, but he chose to walk. He arrives home just as the ambulance attendant is loading his wife into the back of the ambulance.

Another ten years have passed. Bert and Pia have been married for some time now. Bert is in his fifties. They have two daughters. On my rare visits back to England, I have watched Caroline, Jackie's daughter, emerge into a full-fledged personality. She has a mane of thick blond hair, an almost husky yet girlish voice, and the same impish humor as her mother.

Tomorrow, Caroline is coming to visit me in Asheville.

CHAPTER 20A

London, 1953

THE NUMBER SIXTEEN bus route ran down Park Lane. Coming from Oxford Street, I would get off the bus at the Dorchester hotel and take off running to Mum's flat at 49 Hill Street. Prostitutes pretty much lined the streets between the bus stop and home. The reason I ran was not because I was afraid of them but because I thought I might be mistaken for one of them. The only way I could tell who they were was because they just stood there. So I kept moving.

At fifteen I was asked out on my first "date." His name was Charles Clore. I knew him as part of my Jewish teenage group, and because the entire Clore family had a reputation for having "horse faces," this intrigued and amused me. In my parents' social circle, the Clore family was well-known. It so happened that Charles Clore was a philanthropist and financier and one of the wealthiest men in London. But my date was way down in the pecking line, being the son, not *the* Charles Clore. However, just the name was impressive. So when I asked Daddy if I could go on a date, I was shocked when he didn't even ask me with whom.

Charles was to pick me up at Arlington House at six in the evening. Daddy went to the door to let him in. I heard Daddy say, "Hello, Charles, how are you?" I followed my father to be included in the greeting. Daddy said, "Come in for a few minutes. Would you like a drink?"

He poured something for Charles and for himself, and they exchanged pleasantries until Charles said, "I think it's time to go." Daddy got my beautiful emerald-green Bernard and Lakin swing coat, helped me on with it, then put on his coat. The three of us walked to the front door. We waited for the lift, and went down to the parking garage which was beneath the building. The door opened, and Daddy somehow herded us over to his car.

My loving father opened the back door, then motioned for me to get in. Charles then got in beside me in the back.

That was my first date! Daddy even paid for dinner!

CHAPTER 20B

Marriage and Asheville, 1958

FRED USED THE blue-and-white Chevy company car to show me around. As the scenery in North Carolina was new to me, I began to notice large tents with tables and picnic-bench seating, set up in the middle of fields, scattered here and there along the highway. This was my introduction to the term *Bible Belt*. "What's going on there?" I asked Fred.

"That's an evangelist meeting." He answered.

The word *evangelist* was new to me, but not for long. Church meetings of one sort or another dominated the TV. Billy Graham soon became a household word! Even TV automobile commercials sounded to me like a preacher was selling cars; either that or a silky, sweet Southern blond was caressing the merchandise.

When my mother moved to Asheville, fifty years later, she listened to Billy Graham's radio broadcasts regularly. My mother hadn't been exposed to the Christian world as I had. She had a lot to tell him! Firstly, she noted that if Jesus died for their sins, he was being used as a "whipping boy." Whipping boys were hired to take the punishment for rich kids in expensive English prep schools, and soldiers who were paid to fight in place of powerful men; in other words, Jesus was being used as the Lord's gofer—not a flattering picture. My mother would outtalk Billy while he was on the air, "Jesus was gay. Why else would he surround himself with men all the time?"

I'd say, "Mum, you don't have a very high opinion of Jesus, do you?"

And she'd answer, "Jan, I think he was a good man. After all, he was a religious Jew."

Because of Billy Graham's daily dose, Mum and I discussed Jesus a lot. "What is meant by Jesus being Father, Son, and Holy Ghost?" she asked. I couldn't attempt to answer that one, but we agreed that that was a way to give God a human form, instead of the questionable "I am that I am" that we grew up with.

They were in their late seventies when Mum and her husband, Vic, moved from Manhattan to Asheville. They made a handsome vintage pair. They could have been models in a Selfridges window in the 1940s.

Mum managed to keep her vivid colors out there; matching red shoes, matching red bag, stockings every day, and, in fact, red hair, dyed to match a sample, cut directly from a natural redhead who mum had admired so sincerely that the young lady offered it up.

Victor dressed in his dark suit, fedora hat, suitably medium-sized cigar, with a quick word ready on his lips for anyone who came within earshot.

Mum would look up at the mountains and wonder out loud, "What am I doing here?" Her question was answered one day when, after eating lunch out, she and Vic went into Stein Mart. They were asking the lady at the checkout to call a cab, as they needed a ride home.

This was a life-changing moment. A young woman within earshot said, "I can ride you home. Where do you live?"

"Oh, you are too kind. That would be wonderful." Mum's gentle English breeding charmed the world, she was the real thing—a "lady."

Tory Councell, mother of six homeschooled children, took my parents home that day, and became their angel throughout, and by becoming their angel, she became mine.

Mum had brought her furnishings with her from London. Her hand-painted bed was decorated with trumpeting angels reaching to heaven on the oversized headboard. Her bedroom was painted peach to match the furniture.

In the living room, the emerald-green Chinese lacquered desk stood open to show the miniature figures painted inside, against a cream background. Each piece carried memories of weekend treasure hunts on Portobello Road. With the exception of the desk which was given to me for my birthday by one of Mum's male friends! Even the chandelier had hunter-green velvet lampshades. The decor was part elegant British antique and part gypsy bordello.

Tory introduced Mum and Vic to her family, including her husband, John-Mark, and her father and mother-in-law. They all adopted my parents, literally. They took them for Sunday lunches, Sunday concerts, Sunday soirees in people's houses. They swapped life's stories, celebrated birthdays together, and bonded to the point that when Vic died, just short of reaching his hundredth birthday, they came in full mourning to his funeral.

Mum noticed that they spoke of Jesus's life and times and how he saved, sacrificed, and died. They included her in more intimate Sunday gatherings where she learned of Christians who had protected Jews during World War II.

She learned about Corrie Ten Boom who, as a leader overseeing a network of "safe houses" for those hunted by the Gestapo, was imprisoned in Ravensbrück concentration camp. It was estimated she saved the lives of eight hundred Dutch Jews.

They took her for beautiful Sunday car rides. And they took her to The Cove. My ears pricked up at that one.

"Jan, I think they would like me to be Christian. They've been so good to me, I want to please them."

I said, "Mum, you go ahead and become a Christian. I think that is just fine. I promise you, G-d won't mind. Don't worry, I will see to it that you are buried as a Jew."

She smiled. "Thank you, darling."

The Cove is the heartbeat of Billy Graham country.

Mum had come full circle.

CHAPTER 21

And Did Those Feet in Ancient Times

IN 2016, AFTER sixty-plus years, I found myself back in the ornate yet tranquil church of St. Mary's. The school had arranged a special service for current and returning students followed by an open-house tea. The banners of all four saints are paraded through the aisles, passed the pews, in celebration of the returning students and the Battle of Hastings's 1500th anniversary.

The banners have surely shrunk since my school days. I remember being consumed with their dominance in the Abbot's Hall during morning prayers.

My voice joins in the school's anthem as we sing, "Dear Lord and Father of mankind, forgive our foolish ways…" Lauren was determined to witness this. She sits on my right, and, thanks to the internet, Fanny sits on my left. She and I had reunited through the "Battle Axe old girls club." We discovered our mutual search had begun at the same time. Fanny had picked us up at the airport so she could drive us back to her house where we were to spend a couple of nights.

I used the loo as soon as I could. I knew we were in England on first, second, third, and fourth flushing. Nothing had changed. Fanny came to the rescue. She explained how there was a trick to make a successful flush. It was over my head. Yes, it was a chain, but so was the trick to flushing it. I had to ask for her help every time.

At the next house we visited, the bathroom door handle came off in my hand! The most uncanny "cloakroom" was in a hotel. I asked the concierge where it was and was told "over there" as he pointed to a paneled wall that I had just passed. I walked by it again. I asked again. The same response. It was there, but where? Two more passes and I'll give up. But I had to go! This time, I walked with my hand pressed against the wall. Bingo, the wall gave way. By then, my heart was racing, so I purposely left the door ajar for a quick escape.

After the honorary speeches, we are invited to the Abbot's Hall for tea. School teas were never like this spread. Cakes, tarts, sandwiches in every imaginable shape, flavor, and size, from individual to banquet. The common denominator was they were all English—treacle tart, coconut meringue, golden syrup, marzipan-encrusted fruitcake covered in crisp icing, nano-thin-sliced-minus-crust triangular-shaped cucumber, and cream cheese sandwiches. The one thing that was not in my memory bank was the assortment of teas. No English tea-time tea here! I gorged. I made up for the eleven boarding school years of mentally marking my Thursday tea treat as it passed by me, toward the matron manning the table.

It was during tea that a few of the current students mingled with the guests. This was my chance to get the scoop. "What is it like here now?" Nothing but glowing reports on that. "Could I show my daughter the attic that I occupied for a couple of years?"

"Attic?" student rep repeated.

"Yes, I was confined to the attic as my punishment for—"

Her quizzical look stopped my explanation. "Where was it?"

"Up the stairs through the little door at the end of the corridor, then at the top of the curving stone stairs of the turret."

"Oh, I didn't know that leads to an attic, but that area is blocked off. It has been condemned."

"But I have to see it again!"

"I'm sorry."

Knowing that it was still there, even if not available, gave me some closure, and credibility in the eyes of my daughter.

"So, Mum, the banners that were paraded in church, were they new?"

Fanny answers, "No, why do you ask?"

"Because Mum always described them like this." Her arms reach up to the sky, down to the ground, and fully extended.

"Yes, they were…to us. They've shrunk like we have!"

"And what about the driveway, you had to run all the way from here to there?" she said, a quirky smile hovering on her face. She points to the gateway less than twenty feet away.

"Is that it?" Fanny to my rescue again.

"Okay, okay, but it was before breakfast!"

After our tea, we went for a walk through the bower of ewe trees, passed the pigpen—no snorting, grunting pigs anymore—passed the monk's dormitories. The grass tennis courts were updated and the flower gardens trimmed down.

I found myself humming, then the words came. I began to sing, "And we shall build Jerusalem, on England's green and pleasant land." Always my favorite hymn, William Blake knew how to revere England.

The heavy gates clanked open, and I looked back for what I knew would be the last time.

That night we spent with Fanny. The next day, Lauren and I will join Angie and Caroline to celebrate Rosh Hashanah, the Jewish New Year.

I had come full circle.

The End

ANECDOTES ABOUT ELSIE

AS MY DAUGHTER, Lauren, closed the door to my mother's apartment, Lauren said, "Mum, I don't want to freak you out, but Grandma has roaches."

I blanched and asked, "Where?"

"Open a cabinet door in the kitchen."

So my mum wouldn't hear me, I unlocked her front door and sidled into the kitchen. I opened the first cabinet door, but nothing struck me. I started to go back out when something must have caught my eye. I stood perfectly still in front of the open cabinet. The cans on the shelf seemed to be pulsing. I shuddered and left the apartment.

The next day, I sat with Mum at the dining room table. As her right hand lay on the table, I spotted a roach fast-tracking directly toward Mum. I said, "Mum, you have roaches."

She said, "No, I don't," and, still looking directly at me, slammed her hand on top of the unsuspecting villain.

On her way to Switzerland, Mum noticed that the gentleman next to her was traveling light. She said to the customs officer weighing her luggage, "Since we are traveling together, would you mind weighing our luggage together?"

The officer replied, "I would, madam. But you are going to Zurich, and he is going to Paris."

My mum visited my stepfather each day when he was in the nursing home. On one occasion, she had an upset stomach. I received a call from the head nurse.

"Your mother made a mess in the bathroom yesterday. The staff feels that she needs a companion when she visits her husband in the future."

I said, "My mum is here now, so how about I bring her to your staff meeting so you could tell her yourself?" I ran down the hall to fetch Mum and said to her, "Mum, the staff has something to say to you," as I wheeled her toward an open door. The staff were seated around a table.

Mum entered saying, "I've just had an idea that the patients will love. I could visit each room and freshen up their flowers by watering them, removing the—"

"Mum, I believe the staff have something to say to you. Who would like to go first?"

I wheeled Mum over to the nearest nurse, who said, "I think that's a fine idea."

After offering Mum up to each person, we left the room with my heart bursting with admiration…for my mum!

In her nineties, Mum told me about her life during the Blitz. Food rationing was enforced, and one had to register at the local grocery store. It so happened that our local grocery store was Fortnum & Mason. The men who worked there wore evening suits with tails, bow ties, and white gloves.

Mum's volunteer job after a bombing was to match blown-up body parts. She shared this with me once and never spoke of it again.

When Mum died, Angie phoned from England. I told her that Mum's friends were suggesting dresses she would have wanted to wear to be buried in. Her response was, "Janice, your mother was quintessentially Jewish English. She would have wanted to be buried in a shroud." And so she was.

ABOUT THE AUTHOR

JAN WAS BORN in London England. After World War II broke out, she was evacuated to America. It was 1940. She returned to England in 1943. She was immediately sent to Battle Abbey Boarding School, where she stayed for the next eleven years. She passed her joint Oxford-Cambridge GCE A levels early, followed by graduating from the London School of Fashion, then, in 1957, she moved back to America.

She has two adult children and four grandchildren, three surviving.

After a career in radio, Jan authored three books—*Signed with an X, Cat Tails,* and *Asher*—and coauthored two on her adopted hometown of Asheville, North Carolina, where she splits her time with Sarasota, Florida.

CPSIA information can be obtained
at www.ICGtesting.com
Printed in the USA
BVHW091009240122
627022BV00013B/468

9 781662 433931